a hundred
little pieces
on the end
of the world

john rember

a hundred
little pieces
on the end
of the world

University of New Mexico Press | Albuquerque

© 2020 by John V. Rember
All rights reserved. Published 2020
Printed in the United States of America

Library of Congress Cataloging-in-Publication Data

Names: Rember, John, author.

Title: A hundred little pieces on the end of the world / John Rember.

Other titles: 100 little pieces on the end of the world

Description: Albuquerque: University of New Mexico Press, 2020.

Identifiers: LCCN 2019042719 (print) | LCCN 2019042720 (e-book) | ISBN 9780826361356 (cloth) | ISBN 9780826361363 (e-book)

Subjects: LCSH: Civilization, Western—Forecasting.

Classification: LCC PS3568.E5574 H86 2020 (print) | LCC PS3568.E5574 (e-book) | DDC 814.54—DC23

LC record available at https://lccn.loc.gov/2019042719

LC e-book record available at https://lccn.loc.gov/2019042720

Cover and text designed by Mindy Basinger Hill
Composed in Adobe Jenson Pro

for julie,
who casts a soft and
beautiful light

contents

foreword

In December of 1999 Julie and I acted in a play at the Duchess Theatre in London's West End. The play was Michael Frayn's *Copenhagen*. It staged a 1941 meeting between Niels Bohr and Werner Heisenberg. This meeting of those two physicists—first collaborators, then enemies—may or may not have kept the Nazis from developing the atomic bomb.

One of the conceits of *Copenhagen* is that posterity gets to pass judgment on the guilt or innocence of its forebears. To represent that judgment, a jury box formed the back of the stage.

Julie and I had seats in the jury box because we had shown up at the last moment for SRO tickets, and posterity was in short supply that night. We faced the audience. Six feet away were actors representing Bohr and Heisenberg and Bohr's wife, Margrethe, and we watched as they debated their future and our lives.

Our seats were a little public, but once the house lights came down, the rest of the audience was invisible. We put on our best judgmental faces and listened to Frayn's lines as he explored the moral questions of conceiving, constructing, and using atomic weapons.

Copenhagen is a play about uncertainty. Appropriately, we left the theater without a verdict. But since that night I have decided that Werner Heisenberg's most diabolical invention wouldn't have been the atomic bomb even if he had managed to produce twenty of them for his boss.

Instead, it would have remained his Uncertainty Principle. Heisenberg demonstrated that the more you know about where a subatomic particle is, the less you know about where it's going, and vice versa. Put that way, it looks innocuous enough. But the Uncertainty Principle has, as a metaphor, neatly disconnected our past from our present and put our future out of reach. It has made all prediction suspect, all data conditional.

Some symptoms:

Truth exists only within a tribe. Darwinism is revealed as metaphysics. Multiple universes exist for a single entity. Reality does not exist apart from discourse.

Schrödinger's cat might be Schrödinger's dog, or Schrödinger's T. rex. Schrödinger himself might be in his hypothetical box, about to be dead or about to be alive.

There may be more than one box.

I'm describing an evolution faster than the one Darwin had in mind. Contemporary humans are the result of an unnatural selection that has taken place ever since Plato started exploring the void between what he could see and what he could imagine. The extent of that evolution can be seen in the shadowy avatar reflected in the glass of your computer screen.

I write from Sawtooth Valley in central Idaho. Idaho is isolated from most of humanity by dry distance. Sawtooth Valley is isolated from the rest of Idaho by mountains. It's a refuge from which I can watch the feedback loops in global politics, climate, and economies as they approach the steep parts of their exponential curves.

In the pages that follow, I make predictions, but I'm aware the future can't be predicted. I'm trying instead to predict the present, which is difficult enough.

In these hundred short pieces, I've tried to witness the here and now. It has not been easy for someone who used to consider witnessing a low-effort endeavor, one for life's spectators rather than for people like myself, who could, through good will, improve the world.

Of late I've realized how impossible it is to do the right thing once cause and effect has abdicated. Instead I've tried to look at the world from this beautiful if small and temporary place, and to let you in on what I see and hear and think. Put another way, I hope to bring human-scale realities to the readers of this small book.

John Rember
SAWTOOTH VALLEY,
IDAHO, 2019

a hundred
little pieces
on the end
of the world

the way we live now

Life and love after collapse.

1

I know how to harness a horse to a plow. I know how to do basic blacksmithing and welding, pack a horse, shoe the same horse, and use a crosscut saw and broadaxe. I can fell a big tree in a desired direction, wind permitting. I know how to trap beaver, coyote, and muskrat, build a tight log cabin with hand tools and indigenous materials, kill and skin and cut up elk and deer, trim and adjust kerosene lanterns, irrigate, milk a cow, and take care of chickens. I can stay safe and warm while camping in below-zero temperatures and start fires in wet weather. I know basic wilderness medicine and can treat burns, open wounds, and broken legs.

Except for tree-felling every firewood season—with a gas-powered chainsaw—I haven't used these skills in forty years. I don't miss using them. I don't ever want to use them again. Most of them were obsolete when I was born, and I would never have learned them except that when I was three my father quit his life as a hard-rock miner and moved to a small homestead in Sawtooth Valley in central Idaho to become a fishing and hunting guide and trapper.

Our household economy was mostly preindustrial. We kept chickens and packhorses and ate wild game and wild salmon. We heated with firewood, and, until the electrical grid reached us a few years later, we used oil lamps for light.

By the standards of our neighbors and my grade-school classmates, we were poor. My parents had mortgaged our family's future to buy our forty acres. I can remember nights when my parents stayed up late with their ledger, trying to figure out how they could make another seventy-five-dollar monthly payment when the clients were few and the expenses many.

A decade after we had moved to the valley, when the guiding business faltered because of the dam-caused destruction of Idaho's salmon runs, my father contracted to build trails in the Sawtooth Primitive Area, where equipment with wheels wasn't allowed. We had to use packhorses and hand tools and child labor. Child labor was me.

I spent several adolescent summers staring at the back end of a harnessed horse, guiding a one-sided plow, peeling the hillside rocks out and down to make new trail. We were eighteen miles from a road. Our stove was a campfire. Our shower was a five-gallon fire-blackened steel bucket with a showerhead welded to its bottom. We ate fish and canned ham and, after the fresh greens ran out, canned peas, canned beans, and potatoes. Lots of potatoes.

All through those summers, sun-glittering B-52s flew thirty thousand feet above our heads, scattering aluminum chaff that decorated the alpine firs like Christmas tinsel. They reminded us that in a day or less, our tents and kitchen and sleeping cots, our shower bucket and creek-side food cache and even our unfinished trail—these could lose all meaning. The high valley we camped in, full of lakes, waterfalls, mossy meadows, and house-sized blocks of granite, would no longer be home to horse or human. Neither would anyplace else.

When I turned eighteen, old enough to work for the federal government, I became a US Forest Service wilderness ranger and refined my horse-packing and hand-tool skills. I got my EMT certificate. I ski patrolled at the Sun Valley ski resort during college vacations.

My seasonal jobs paid my tuition, which illustrates how long ago I attended college. After graduation I quit the Forest Service and the ski patrol and began teaching English in a small private school in Sun Valley. I left teaching to write a cardiology-for-laymen book. After that I went back to school for a graduate degree that allowed me to teach English literature and magazine journalism at the College of Idaho, a small liberal-arts college forty miles west of Boise.

During my first few years of teaching college I published personal essays in a local arts weekly, one of them about being sixteen and stuck out in a wilderness where my closest friends were my horse and my Pulaski. I confessed that what I really wanted was to be a lifeguard at the Sun Valley Lodge pool. It didn't matter that I couldn't swim.

It didn't matter what I really wanted, either. I wasn't lifeguarding. I was working long summer days in dust and heat and mosquitos. For recreation I took to naming minor Sawtooth peaks and trees and waterfalls after my previous school year's crushes. I hadn't yet realized that starting a first-day-of-school conversation with, "I named a tree after you," didn't qualify as a social skill.

It was a bittersweet essay, and after it was published I received a bittersweet letter from a young woman who described growing up lonely on a cattle ranch in eastern Oregon, fifty miles from any highway. She described high school summers of yearning to sit by a municipal pool, talking and laughing with friends, and getting a tan. Instead, she spent her school vacations moving cattle on a skittish horse, fighting gnats and horseflies and sunburn, surrounded on all sides by a sagebrush-fringed horizon.

It was a letter that changed my life. In subsequent conversations its author and I discovered that neither of us would get on a horse again if we could help it, and that neither of us saw value in rejecting the comforts of technology. Both of us preferred contemporary industrial civilization to its alternative, however romantic that alternative might appear to people who hadn't lived through it. Both of us felt, in retrospect, that our alienated adolescences had given us essential adult strengths, but we were certain there were easier ways to get them.

We discovered other things in common, including a weakness for lounging around the pools of hot-springs resorts—as long as they didn't make you ride their horses—but it was our differences that caused us to marry each other a few years later. Julie's still a sweet young thing, at least in my eyes, and I'm not, but between my caution and experience and her energy and enthusiasm we've made it twenty-seven good years together. We love each other without reservation, is one way to put it. We laugh a lot, is another.

For many of those years, we earned two salaries. No kids. We paid off our house and cars and put one of our salaries into savings. We might still be in those jobs, saving and slaving away, except for the 2000 presidential election, which brought George Bush and Dick Cheney to power. That election caused us to look critically at our careers, at the institutions we worked for, at the people whose judgment we trusted, and where the next decades might find us.

The country itself began to resemble a decaying stage set. Some of my students were going deep into debt to pay for their college degrees, and I knew that without luck and sacrifice and more luck, that debt was going to stay with them for life. Older faculty colleagues began showing the stress of their jobs in their bodies and faces, and they began questioning how they had spent their lives. One of them, at his retirement party, turned to me and said, "If there's one thing I learned in forty years of teaching, it's that institutions don't love you back."

My parents, still on their place in Sawtooth Valley, were old enough to need help with their everyday life. Their age and frailty, when they had always seemed powerful, decisive, and independent, reminded us that our own independence was limited. We needed to spend it in ways that were full of meaning, or, because meaning itself was starting to seem fragile, full of days fixing fences or cutting firewood, shoveling snow and cleaning irrigation ditches, replacing logs in the walls of old cabins—to pay obeisance to the real, in any way we could think of doing it.

Fifteen years ago, not knowing how long the world would last, but thinking it wasn't going to last long, we left our careers, sold our house, bought annuities, and retreated to a cabin I had built on my parents' place. We turned our jobs into long-distance electronic endeavors, and the hit we took in income was less than what we saved in expenses.

We don't have a garden because it still frosts some summer nights. We can't watch broadcast TV, but we do have broadband and a Netflix subscription. We have an old pickup for firewood, an old SUV for winter roads, and a not-so-old car that gets decent gas mileage, an essential thing here in the valley, where there is no public transportation and likely never will be.

Except for a frantic two-and-a-half-month tourist season every summer, we live more or less by ourselves. My parents, now gone for a decade, lived as long as they could in a place they loved, and they serve as our example.

Isolation is the price we pay. Our community is geographically gated. In the dark days of winter there are maybe a hundred people in our surrounding hundred square miles. We don't go outside unless it's above ten below. Some days we don't go outside at all, because inside are good books and a warm fire and tea water boiling in the kettle atop the stove.

On sunny winter days we walk to the hill on the other side of the highway, put on our backcountry skis and skins, and climb the eight hundred vertical feet to the top. We ski deep powder on good days, breakable crust on bad days.

Lately, instead of buying gold or silver as some of our neighbors urge us to do, we've been visiting warmer places when the days get short, only returning home once the sun starts moving north on the horizon.

Neither Julie nor I grew up middle class, but we backed into its lower childless reaches, just when the rest of America's middle class—and its world—started to unravel.

3

Not long after we moved to Sawtooth Valley, I started writing a column for a paper in Ketchum, the small tourist town that fills the space between Sun Valley Resort and its ski mountain. Tourism is a delicate business, subject to economic or climatic catastrophe, and my column became a forum for apocalyptic musings.

For some time I had been an *après moi le deluge* guy, although for me the deluge wasn't nuclear, biological, or chemical. I had simply observed that screens were replacing real life in the lives of my students. They were getting good, expensive educations, but I wasn't sure they would be able to connect them with anything of substance.

That, and the fact that in our government and corporate

boardrooms it more and more looked as if the folks who obeyed their basest impulses were running the country. The people who operated according to reason and careful observation didn't think they could run anything but their own lives, and maybe not even those.

I called my column *End Notes*, because I could Google "End of Days" any day of the week and have my pick of two million or so separate dooms to write about. Jesus was riding in at the head of an angel SWAT team, or a fourteen-mile-long asteroid was about to crash into Los Angeles, or the Star-spawn of the Dread Cthulhu was at last rising out of the Marianas Trench. These things were fun to write about and fun to make fun of, but after a year or so the Doom of the Month Club turned mean. Lots of the doomsayers I was reading were not delusional ranters. They were sober social critics, economists, historians, and climate scientists.

These experts became more and more compelling as time went on. Once we had moved to Sawtooth Valley, it became apparent how vulnerable Julie and I remained to the civilization from which we had physically removed ourselves.

Our savings would become worthless. The electricity would go out. Gasoline and propane would disappear down an energy-return-on-energy-invested dry hole. We'd freeze to death, unshowered, in the dark. We'd succumb to heat stroke on a summer night when the wet-bulb temperature stayed above 37°C. Marauding hordes, escaping wrecked cities on bicycles, would shoot us as we fled out the door of our cabin, which they had set on fire to get at the canned goods in our crawl space.

We would die before our time, in other words. So would a lot of other people. Probably all in the same two or three months, given the speed of decline that some people—historians, mostly—expected.

Our humor wasn't gallows humor, but it was tumbrel

humor. "I'm in favor of marauding hoards," I said. "Let the caches of food, gold, and ammo come to us."

4

During my career as a professor, a colleague in the psychology department was married to a survivalist. She would lecture all day on the basal ganglia, the limbic system, and the amygdala and then go home, where her husband's reptile brain had caused him to bury a Quonset hut in the backyard and stock it with freeze-dried food, fuel, a chemical toilet, thousands of flashlight batteries, and tens of thousands of rounds of ammo. Faculty wits used to speculate that their sex life was better than their conversation.

When I spoke with Julie about my concern that our savings might not outlast our lives, that we might need ten years' worth of freeze-dried food, that I was thinking about purchasing a small arsenal for under the bed—nothing special, you understand, just an M-14, a samurai sword, and some mail-order pathogens—she said, "If civilization collapses, I don't want to live. Not in an overshot world in the midst of a die-off, even if we have a fully-equipped bunker to live in, even with solar power, even with a geothermal greenhouse, even with weapons that could depopulate half of Idaho."

It's a shock when the person you love tells you they don't want to make it through the coming bottleneck. It means one solid choice is to become a victim of circumstance.

But it also sparks a round of honest thinking, and out of that honest thinking comes the realization that in the long run, we're all victims of circumstance. All of us are hostage to a civilization that, judging from what it's doing to our habitat, doesn't love us back. A corollary: some of us will leave that unloving relationship.

5

If you're going to be a victim of circumstance, having an old pump shotgun and fifty rounds of buckshot will do you just fine as an arsenal. When the marauding orphan horde—I fear they will look a lot like the wandering orphans of Stalin's Russia, whose kulak parents had disappeared in the purges— when that horde of murderous unschooled children shows up at your door, you can take out a couple of them before they get you. That will temporarily discourage them from attacking your neighbors.

But in the long run, numbers, mobility, and a hunger-fueled lack of compassion are going to be on their side. They're going to get your neighbors, too. They won't have the same reverence for the aged and educated that we aged and educated folks have.

6

When people say that a kill-or-be-killed life won't be worth living, they have reached that conclusion after carefully examining the realities of collapse for their own lives and the lives of the people around them.

That's where Julie and I find ourselves now, even with lives that have been happier and longer than expected. A happy old age is still possible for us, but only if something that is demonstrably killing the planet—industrial civilization, with its global CO_2 emissions, estrogen-mimicking plastics, toxic financial systems, private security companies, trash-filled ocean gyres, earth-sterilizing agribusinesses, deep-ocean oil blowouts, ministries of tourism, autobahns, jumbo jets, and periodic nuclear accidents—keeps on keeping on. Business as usual might be good news when you're hoping to live twentieth-century lifespans in a twenty-first-century environment, but it's bad news for people who love their grandchildren. They can only hope that their grandchildren will, when all is said and done, love them back.

7

It goes against my nature to become a victim of circumstance. I've been going through my parents' storage sheds, inventorying harnesses, horse collars, hand tools, wood stoves, nails, traps, and fishing gear. I bought a .22 rifle with a scope, because at my age my eyes can either see open sights or a target but not both. I had my old chainsaw overhauled because I'd happily pay five beaver pelts for a gallon of saw gas rather than go back to a crosscut saw to get in a winter's firewood. I'm accumulating lightweight camping gear just in case Julie and I need to spend a few safer-than-at-home nights in the nearby hills.

It will be better if things fall apart in deep winter. I know from my early life in this valley that people can live without electricity. You'll have to keep a stove going 24/7 in January. Without a cache of food in the crawl space, you'll have to kill a large animal or a lot of small ones to get to April. It'll be work just to stay warm. You won't have much time left over for movies or dinners out, even if the high passes weren't drifted shut.

But there will be books, and candles, and berries, and dried mushrooms. Small joys, but joys, at least for a time. These are what you think about when you think about survival, in a good way.

8

Several summers ago an executive of the company Julie works for called us up from the lodge at Redfish Lake, a nearby six-mile-long glacial pool. He wanted to take us for a boat ride. He picked us up at the dock in a twenty-foot aluminum jet boat powered by a Ford 360 cubic-inch v8, a motor that would get nine miles per gallon when it was installed in an F-150, maybe five when powering a boat. It had leather upholstery, cupholders, a convertible top, a weather station, and depth gauge. Because it was a calm afternoon, we could cruise at fifty miles per hour on the glassy swells of the lake. *Eat your heart out, Thorstein Veblen*, I thought.

We roared by the shore, leaving canoeists and kayakers struggling to stay upright in our wake. We shot between fishermen and their bobbers and violently rocked a little houseboat anchored in a peaceful cove.

I silently drank an oaky Australian chardonnay and waved at people in other powerboats, checked out the large white sunbathers stranded on the beach, ate hummus and chips, and hung my head out into the clear, cool wind. When we had finished weaving around the lake, the odometer indicated we had gone 22.5 miles. We had just burned enough gas to cut a winter's worth of firewood.

We said good-bye to our host. As the boat roared off, the beach, the trees, the lake, the water-skiers and sunbathers, and the boat's owner and his wife flashed sepia in my eyes. They became an old cardboard-mounted photograph, cracked at the edges and shakily focused on a world long dead.

9

Even though no one can predict the future, everyone can imagine it. Here's what I imagine Julie and I will witness in the months before we die: The electricity will go out in cities here and there in these not-so-United States. Gasoline will disappear from gas stations, leaving once-wealthy suburbanites stranded in their great rooms, heating canned soup on chef-sized gas ranges in their granite kitchens, looking out at lawns yellowed by drought. National Guard troops handing out government rations will be a staple of the evening news.

Here in Idaho, the Mormon Church will provide a measure of cultural stability, even for us Gentiles in its midst. For a longer time than in other parts of the country, our lights will go on at night because of Northwest hydro and wind power.

Some folks in the valley plan to occupy geographical choke points and turn away refugees, some of them with non-feral children in tow.

The habit of exchanging things of value for hundred-dollar bills will persist as long as most people believe in magic.

The brutal repression of mobs by military force will happen elsewhere, but it will be shown to us. The counter-revolution *will* be televised, and we'll have a government consisting of military men dressed as civilians.

Think turning off power and water as a political measure. Think internal passports. Think martial-law tribunals. The United States of America will exist, but God help anyone who demands the protection of its Bill of Rights.

We will have victory gardens. Strategic-metal drives. The government will own TV networks. It will not be good to have anything worth stealing, by lawyers or banks or thieves.

10

Back when I turned sixty-two, I signed up for Social Security. It was a surprising and disturbing rite of passage, not easily defused by humor. But I joked that it was as close as I would ever get to receiving a MacArthur Grant. I joked that I'd been hoping all my life to get money back from the government, which had never been a sure thing. I joked that it was going to be all fun tickets and not all cat food, not with money still in the bank, not with the bank still standing, not with the dollar a recognized currency.

These are not really jokes.

I figured that I'd sign up at age sixty-two rather than waiting for sixty-six, because I wasn't sure if by the time I reached sixty-six the retirement age wouldn't be seventy, and if I waited until then—you get the idea. I also worried that I would outlast our government's willingness to put funds in my bank account every month—I worried that I would outlast our government, come to think of it—so I got in while getting in was still a thing.

That was the good news. The bad news was that old age, which for most of my life was safely distant, had arrived on my doorstep. It wasn't carrying an AR-15, but it smiled an evil smile that suggested it was going to kill me anyway.

Julie and I both have Alzheimer's in our families, and at least if civilization goes away neither of us will end our days hallucinating the past in a nursing home. The saying goes that there are no pockets in the shroud, which usually is taken to mean you can't take your money with you. After taking care of a parent with Alzheimer's, I've realized there are also no pockets for what remains among the living. What you possess in the grave has to have preceded you there.

It's a short imaginative journey from taking care of a parent with Alzheimer's to thinking we live in a civilization with Alzheimer's, if the insistent cultural belief in a long-disappeared world is any indication.

If civilization comes to an end, I won't mind getting back to hard physical work, because it generally kills you prior to assisted living, no matter what you eat. As a writer who researched heart disease, I know hearts don't last forever. As a cement worker between bouts of teaching, I witnessed what the old guys on the crew looked and acted like, and how many painkillers they ate.

Here's the death I've come to prefer: one day I'll be packing a mule, or chasing a deer, or shoeing a horse, or pouring cement—and I'll just fall over. It's not the worst way to die when you go out deeply focused on the work you're doing, especially if it's keeping other people alive.

I worry about dying before Julie, even though she is more capable and self-sufficient than most people. I keep offering to buy her a pink .38 revolver for her birthday, but she refuses to learn to use it. When we first got together, I joked about her throwing herself on my funeral pyre, which caused her to joke about running off with the strong young guy who had built the funeral pyre.

But lately she's been saying, "It's been a good life with you. I don't want it to end. It's a beautiful world. I don't want it to end, either. I love both you and the world, and if I could make our adventure last and last, I would."

"Forever?"

"Forever would get boring. But for a good long time."

I think more about my death when she's talking like this than I do when she's talking about my death.

I wish I had faith in a sustainable future—my own and everybody else's. I wish Julie and I had a good long time in front of us, but we—and civilization—started borrowing time long ago. I wish I still believed in the persistence of civilization, especially if that civilization was one that could stop putting carbon in the air and oil in the oceans and destroying forests and farmland and fresh water and making munitions out of depleted uranium.

I wish I had faith in a human nature that would allow my generation to make choices for the benefit of its children instead of following the rules of buying and selling humans laid down by its great-great-grandparents.

I wish I had the courage to live each day like Julie does. She worries less than I do, and she knows that life is worth living until it isn't.

Seeing the world through her courageous eyes, I've realized that there are other ways of living than brooding darkly on the Second Law of Thermodynamics.

She shows me that with enough courage, you can accept the persistence of entropy. You can understand that the person you love will do well for herself until she doesn't, and that our civilization did well for itself until it didn't.

Not happy realizations, but necessary ones if we're going to turn honest faces to each new day as it arrives in this world.

a few rocks from the box

Any hypothesis can be overturned by new data.
There's always new data.

1

In my sophomore year at Harvard College I enrolled in a
course that had given generations of students a painless way
to satisfy the liberal-arts science requirement. It was known as
Rocks for Jocks, and the final exam was known to be the easy
identification of every rock in a box. If you were an English
Literature major, and you wanted an A in the required science
course, you took geology.

But on the first day of geology class, a new professor
announced that the old Rocks for Jocks was extinct. The Arts
and Sciences faculty were determined to bring rigor into the
geology program. We were in a science class, he said. He was
going to teach us real science, no matter what had been taught
in the past.

The final exam had nothing to do with a box. It asked for
a coherent analysis of the chemistry and resulting crystal
structures of basaltic minerals on a spectrum of temperatures
and pressures. I was surprised and grateful for the B-minus I
received.

Along the way I had been drilled on high-temperature
physics and the dynamics of dissolved gasses, and how alu-
minosilicate, with its strong chemical bonds, makes country

rock hang together. I can still tell you about the relationship between plagioclase and orthoclase, information I haven't used in fifty years.

Other aspects of the course have become more important as I've grown older. The professor was the paleontologist Stephen Jay Gould, who delighted us with lectures on why Godzilla and King Kong would die of heat stroke before they wrecked a single city, and why Mothra wouldn't be able to fly unless the atmosphere had the density of water.

Much later, when I read Gould's *The Mismeasure of Man*, a book that examined the deadly misuse of science to promote unjust social, political, and educational policy, his sentences echoed the clear thinking, humor, and honest approach to the world that had brought the realities of classical physics into his paleontology lectures.

Later in his career Gould went beyond classical physics and applied chaos theory to paleontology. He developed a refinement of evolutionary theory known as punctuated equilibrium. Punctuated equilibrium, put much too simply, suggests that species stabilize for millions of years until climate change causes a mass extinction. What we, as outside observers, perceive as a periodic flowering of species is simple natural selection operating in a world of empty ecological niches. Ten million years after a mass extinction, the earth has a whole new zoo.

Climate change is *always* what causes mass extinctions, if climate change includes asteroid impacts, supervolcanic eruptions, the sudden sublimation of methane clathrates into atmospheric methane, and the appearance of capitalist hominids.

The theory of punctuated equilibrium has been accepted by most evolutionary scientists. However, if Gould were alive today, he'd be subjecting it to his own scientific skepticism. He used science to undermine pseudoscientific certainty, magical thinking about technology, and the dishonest appropriation of scientific metaphors by non-scientists. But he questioned his own work just as much as he questioned the work of less careful people who also called themselves scientists.

The scientific method is just a powerful way to process data, Gould told us. Anyone who makes a religion of science doesn't understand it. Certainty isn't the point. Asking the right questions is the point. Any hypothesis can be overturned by new data, and there's always new data.

In college I came to believe in a method, rather than in the data it processed. I learned to believe in clear and careful thinking. I learned the value of doubt in scenarios marked by aggressive avowals of faith. I learned that humor and humility were essential to science. After I had passed the new version of Rocks for Jocks, it was hard for me to believe didactic scientific pronouncements, especially ones posing as settled truth.

If all this sounds deeply ambiguous, it is. To bring science into any controversy is to introduce shades of gray forbearance where once all was foam-at-the-mouth black and white. But while the scientific method is slow and cannot predict the future, if you'd like to see through the cloud of bullshit generated by bought-and-paid-for experts, it provides useful optics.

Clear thinking. Doubt. Honest approach to the world. Humor. Humility. Science needed all five to function, and, I found out, so did I.

2

After college I started working as a medical writer and had almost finished a book on heart attacks before the company I was working for went broke. For six months I had read medical textbooks and peer-reviewed cardiology journals and talked to cardiologists. I knew a bunch about the human heart and what could go wrong with it.

I also knew about the impossibility of designing adequate study parameters and interpreting results. Briefly put, you can never identify all the causes of a heart attack. You can never identify all the effects of a drug on a human heart or on the life it sustains.

So you can have the famous Framingham Heart Study, which has tracked forty thousand people over three generations, identifying as many risk factors for heart disease as possible, and when all the data is in you'll find that major risk factors are still being identified. Other well-established risk factors are not as risky as they were once thought to be. Previous generations of researchers, working with reams of hard information, came to the wrong conclusion about a diet, drug, or procedure.

The clearest result of the Framingham Study is the ongoing demonstration that any study, no matter how carefully designed, is forever subject to new interpretations. Framingham Study data will be mined again and again by teams of people using ever more sophisticated analyses to promote their competing hypotheses.

3

So, to the present. Gould is seventeen years dead of adenocarcinoma of the lung metastasized to the brain. I mention his cause of death in such detail because he didn't die of abdominal mesothelioma, with which he had been diagnosed twenty years earlier.

Mesothelioma is a disease still considered a quick death sentence. It's an ironic possibility that Gould had contracted it from one of the large blocks of asbestos fibers that were used as teaching aids in college geology labs back in the day. I remember watching a geology lab assistant peel a long feathery fiber from one of those blocks and wave it at us while lecturing on crystal structure. "You can make clothes from these crystals," he said.

Those crystals killed tens of thousands of people. For a long time—as a civilization, anyway—we just didn't know. Evidence exists that the asbestos industry did know but kept its knowledge secret. But as a civilization that holds industrial progress as evidence of grace, we still lack the ability to name or even to conceive of the unthinking evil that has underpinned the culture of resource extraction during the nineteenth, twentieth, and twenty-first centuries.

Evil is the right word here. You might see evil as the product of careful malign intention, but it's rare when that happens. Smart students of evil bet on a lack of thinking every time.

During his reign in Spain, Generalissimo Francisco Franco sent his political enemies to work in mercury mines, where they lasted an average of eighteen months before succumbing to blindness, paralysis, and madness. However repellent that practice was, it could be comprehended as part of the murderous civil war that brought Franco to power.

But when the dying miners in Libby, Montana, were presented with evidence that working in the Libby asbestos mine had given them mesothelioma, many of them refused to believe that the company they had worked for all their lives hadn't been as devoted to them as they had been to it and had in fact known of the hazards of asbestos long before they had been hired.

In his later writings Gould demolished the cover that so-called scientific experts provided for malignant technologies, but that has not kept corporations from continuing to employ science PhDs to testify that lethal products and procedures are safe.

4

"By the summer of 2025," is the opening phrase of a chapter in a history that will be written in 2050, should anyone be around to write it. I'd love to read the rest of that sentence right now, but the nature of future history involves a tedious waiting for verification. Here are some guesses:

".. . world population had hit 8.5 billion."

".. . atmospheric concentrations of CO_2 had reached 457 parts per million."

".. . agricultural production was in steep decline over broad areas of the western, southwestern, and central United States."

".. . Dr. Weltentod had been retired from bioweapons work for twenty years. Alzheimer's was making him paranoid and isolated. But the freezer in his basement was still humming away. The samples he had taken from the lab decades earlier were still viable."

You can have fun doing this sort of thing, but you won't be much wiser for it.

It's not easy to figure out what's determinant in our lives while we're living them. Still, in the here and now, shadows are stirring. The kind of curves that you see in catastrophe theory monographs are beginning to correspond to the activities of the energy, education, and finance industries. We can surmise that these curves will end in catastrophe.

I'd like to know when. I won't find out in time. One of the characteristics of a catastrophic curve is that by the time you recognize it, it's too late.

5

Military historians point out that generals who study the last war to fight the next one end up losing. The study of history is a poor way to predict the future, especially when the time frame of human civilization—in paleontological terms—is statistically insignificant.

That doesn't mean that humans aren't changing things. They are. The time frame of the asteroid impact that wrecked the dinosaurs was statistically insignificant, too.

I'd like to talk to a future historian, because any one of them, by definition, is going to be more reliable than a prophet. Still, there are prophets who seem worth listening to and prophets who seem less so, and if you're going to be one of the ones who is listened to it's better to have common sense than a belief in your own clairvoyance. For one thing, you'll confine your predictions to the present.

Common sense has its pitfalls. It's the complex dark brother of empiricism, and it has none of the authority of science. It's a blend of intuition, instinct, received knowledge, and perception melted together in the crucible of individual will. It can desert you when you most need it. Still, it's helpful to apply it to the world we live in, because it travels farther and faster than science, and it is the source of the occasional rare, out-of-left-field hypothesis, the hypothesis that, once expressed, seems all too true.

For example, if you take a planet with a history of climate phase changes and introduce huge amounts of carbon dioxide and methane into its atmosphere, you're going to get a climate phase change, a transformation where even if the original parameters were to be restored, conditions can never return to what they were. For one thing, a bunch of species will be extinct.

Common sense also suggests that tinkering with genes generates ugly unintended consequences. In a minor example, monarch butterflies are headed for extinction (I should note that it's a minor example unless you're a monarch butterfly) because of the success of crops genetically engineered to resist herbicide. Milkweed, the butterflies' food source, hasn't been engineered to resist herbicides, and it's being poisoned, and the monarchs are starving.

Common sense tells us that human civilization, depending as it does on an increasingly complicated infrastructure, will crash rather than gently decline. The crash will result from the human habit of solving problems by adding a fragile complexity rather than a durable simplicity, or the other human habit of responding to tough times not with common sense but with violence.

And common sense tells us that our ongoing wars will never have happy cost-benefit ratios unless you discount the value of human life to zero. Fortunately for the people who make their money on war, that discount is applied at the cash register. But what's fortunate for them is unfortunate for the people living those worthless lives, their worthlessness made explicit when they end in war.

The scientific method is too slow and too easily challenged to have an impact on these and a bunch of other urgent matters.

6

If Stephen Jay Gould were alive today, he'd be angry. A lifetime of debunking, and what does he get for it?

A parade of expert witnesses in front of Congressional committees, contradicting each other but nonetheless reinforcing Congress's naïve faith in pseudoscience.

In the public mind, an equating of science and technology, when in fact these have little in common and often conflict with each other.

A medical industry so eager to prolong and profit from life that it's redefined life so as to prolong and profit from *something*.

The exploitation of scientific uncertainty by unscrupulous corporations.

The willingness of Americans to leave the present and return, via magical thinking, to a golden time when one could still project one's self into the future in the form of laughing grandchildren.

7

My thoughts are darkening with age. I'm tipping toward techno-nihilism. But it's not the fault of the scientific method. Rather, it's a result of reading the last five or ten years of *New York Times* headlines, and a recent rereading of the old French social critic Jacques Ellul. In his book *The Technological Society*, Ellul makes a strong argument that technology exists as a force in itself, one indistinguishable from death.

Of course, Ellul is no scientist in the mold of Stephen Jay Gould. He's a humorless Jesuit anarchist with literal-minded translators, but he's worth reading if only because he knew enough back in 1960 not to divide technology into Bad (the Bomb) and Good (television, interstate highways, nuclear power plants, the new wonder drug Thalidomide). He declared a pox on all the houses of technology, no matter how shiny and convenient, calling the worship of technology a threat to human liberty and consciousness, even when it didn't immediately burn, cripple, or anesthetize.

If Ellul were alive today, he'd look at texting adolescents, drone surveillance, cyber-terrorists, and medical billing departments, and he would be grimly satisfied at getting a front-row seat at civilization's auto-da-fé.

Here's an Ellul-inspired thought experiment that suggests things could be a good deal worse. If safe and easy-to-construct water-fueled fusion plants could be built in every community, and if a quickly-rechargeable AAA battery could be made to power a vehicle for four hundred miles between charges, we could have the years since 1914, with their limitless economic horizons and millions of war dead, all over again.

8

The depth psychologist Carl Jung said that it's hard to see the lion that has eaten you. But if you're open to your perceptions, you can at least tell that you've been eaten, and by a lion.

The trouble with metaphors like Jung's is that they are reductive. These days, the lion can be the petroleum industry, pharmaceutical capitalism, investment banks, college loans, salvation through technology, fundamentalist ideologies (e.g., salvation through technology), Facebook, or golf—anything that consumes your consciousness and redefines your world in its own terms.

But it doesn't matter what the lion is. If it eats you, you're going to end up as lion shit.

9

Chaos theory has given us a phrase—"a sensitive dependence on initial conditions"—that allows a look into the mechanics of ecosystems, evolution, and the climate. A butterfly's wing-beat—or the lack of it—that causes a tornado ten days later and half a world away, a chance cosmic ray that rearranges a gene, and a mammal that crosses a newly formed land bridge between the placental and marsupial Americas—these things achieve a down-the-line importance out of proportion to their size. In other words, the past is never past, it's woven into every molecule of the present. Yet another way to put it is that you never can identify all the tipping points ahead of time.

Rocks for Jocks was one of my initial conditions, and over the years it has become a larger part of my life than three fifty-year-old credits fulfilling a liberal-arts science requirement. I've become sensitive to whether or not a worldview depends on happy lies and happy liars. I've come to see science as a fundamentally moral endeavor that not all scientific careers fulfill. When anyone says they're basing public policy on science I reach for my copy of *The Mismeasure of Man*.

I also find myself liking the idea of rigor a great deal more than I did when I was a college sophomore. Rigor means you stick with available data and try not to jump to conclusions the data doesn't support. Rigor discourages nostalgic pasts and utopian futures. Rigor makes magical thinking impossible, and that's a good thing if you want to have an intellect worthy of the name.

Rigor makes it possible to understand that our planet is experiencing one of its great extinctions. Habitat loss, warming and acidifying oceans, industrial and agricultural pollution, and suddenly rising levels of methane in the Arctic are putting some punctuation in our equilibrium.

Gould lived long enough to see the beginnings of the current extinction. He didn't flinch from it—that's part of being rigorous—but he didn't take pleasure in it. He had resisted extinction on a personal basis when diagnosed with mesothelioma, and his fascination with the diversity of life suggests he would not have been happy about the disappearance of a single species, much less millions of them.

However, he would have observed that the mechanisms of diversity, which come into play whenever an empty ecological niche presents itself, are being freed from sixty million years of constraints. He might have noted that the current release of trapped methane into the atmosphere parallels a much slower release that occurred 240 million years ago, when 96 percent of ocean species and 70 percent of land vertebrates died out.

As the careful scientist he was, he would have resisted the temptation to say that the same thing is happening now, since there's no need to come to conclusions this early in the experiment. The world is fully engaged in a definitive study of Gould's evolutionary theories, and enormous amounts of data are going to come in over the next ten million years.

Even so, I think Gould would have found it tempting, had he lived ten or twenty years longer, to look at human civilization and see one of those impossible monsters he entertained us with back in Rocks for Jocks—a great misshapen and grotesque mass of slime and teeth climbing out of the sea, shambling toward a city, crushing cars and trucks under its staggering feet, toppling monuments and tossing skyscrapers aside in a drunken delirious rush before finally collapsing exhausted, its bones breaking under its own weight, the heat of its own metabolism—with nowhere to go in all that struggling mass—frying its nerves and congealing its tiny brain.

10

Stephen Jay Gould found joy in a new rock or fossil or previously unremarked feature of petrified anatomy. Any of these things placed him on the edge of the unknown, where all certainty was in danger of being overthrown. He was comfortable and happy and clear-eyed in that place.

When he was diagnosed with mesothelioma, he saw himself again at the brink of the unknown. He lasted there for far longer than expected, twenty years on the scalpel-edge of death, noting, in passing, that you had no need to believe in statistics if you were an individual cancer patient. As a species facing extinction, we can find a rare bit of cheer in his example.

when darkness casts
a hard and pitiless light

A mind is a slippery thing to waste.

1

One of my best writing students ever was a seventh-grader named Darrel. I forget Darrel's family name, but that doesn't matter, because Darrel is the author of the Frank and Dave stories, and that's accomplishment enough to let him go through life in mononymity, like Elvis or Cher or Oprah, or Frank and Dave for that matter. Frank and Dave stories had titles like *Frank and Dave Go Fishing and Catch a Fish*, or *Frank and Dave Push the Explorer Back onto Its Wheels, Change the Tire and Get Back on the Road*, or *Frank and Dave Watch the Super Bowl and Their Team Wins*.

When a Frank and Dave story fulfilled the promise of its title, it ended. There wasn't a lot of conflict in these stories, but they all got to where they said they would go. Frank and Dave weren't complex literary characters, but they liked each other and helped each other out when the fish stopped biting or a tire blew or the opposing team was up by two touchdowns at the half. Good things happened in a Frank and Dave story, and they happened in short, simple sentences full of concrete nouns and action verbs. A lecture I used to give in my graduate-level creative writing classes was called *How to Write Like Darrel*.

But Darrel's greatest asset as a writer was not his simple, clear, and effective language. It was his world. Darrel's parents had raised him in a disciplined but loving environment. They celebrated his successes, and when he failed they reassured him that he would do better next time, and then they analyzed his failure and actively prepared him to succeed. If Darrel behaved badly in class I had only to mention that behavior in a parent-teacher conference and it never happened again.

The world that Darrel lived in was defined by his parents' story, which had them making a lot of money in the stock market and then retiring to a ski resort in their forties and raising a child in a rational, firm, and loving way. When Darrel sat down to write a Frank and Dave story, he was telling yet another version of his life, where success was always the punch line.

Reading a Frank and Dave story did not make me wish for more action or that a really serious bad guy would show up or that the wrong team would lose the big game. Instead, it allowed me to visit a completely safe and grammatical world and to want to get back to that world whenever Darrel handed in another assignment. I gave Darrel an A in seventh-grade English.

If you're wondering how soon I'm going to tell you that Darrel's parents went through divorce and bankruptcy and addiction and criminal prosecution for duct-taping Darrel to the wall on club nights, that's your world view, not mine.

As far as I know, Darrel turned out all right, even if he didn't continue as a writer. And his parents lived into their eighties with their marriage and story intact. They died believing in their story, which isn't the worst way to go.

2

I'm not going to die believing in my story. It's got too many holes in it, too many false starts, too many conflicting plot lines. Not enough meaning. No moral. It's not set in a safe world.

If my story had come into one of my classes, I would have criticized it for having a happy ending in a world lacking happy endings. "Your narrative character has taken himself out of the setting," I would tell the author. "You can't do that."

At the start of every workshop, I used to tell my students the one thing they couldn't say about someone else's work was, "You can't do that." But still.

"He has done nothing to earn the sort of happiness you've thrust upon him," I would say. "And he certainly doesn't deserve to be loved."

Give nonfiction a narrative line, and you've done cosmetic surgery on the real. It only improves things sometimes.

A witness gazing at this process is an author's enemy. When your skull is home to both witness and narrator, they start to bicker and you lose sleep.

I've been waking up at 3:00 a.m. and remembering things I've done that I wish I had done differently, or not at all.

I wish I hadn't called Corinna J. a weirdo when she was sitting at lunch in the Ketchum Elementary School cafeteria when I was twelve and she was thirteen. Corinna *was* a weirdo, and later in life an incredibly attractive and interesting one, but after teaching eighth-graders I've realized that nobody that age should be called a weirdo if you don't want them to remember it for life and to remember, also for life, that you were the one who called them a weirdo.

In sixth grade I shouldn't have made fun of Randy and

LeeAnn E., who lived in a condemned house and wore second-hand clothes and would eat any of your Ketchum Elementary lunch you didn't want, no matter what foul thing the cooks had served up.

I shouldn't have deliberately tripped Roger M. as he ran around a blind corner of the school on his way in from recess when he was a first grader and I was a third grader, because up to that time he'd been a happy little kid, and afterward he was a not so happy little kid who ran the other way when he saw me.

There are many, many more terrible things there in the elementary school memory bank, and I call them up, with a love indistinguishable from masochism, one by one. I'm usually too sleepy by daylight to jump forward to later transgressions, to recall my parents' car that I wrecked or awkward blind dates where I failed to talk much about anything other than recent developments in nuclear physics. Or selfishness-wrecked relationships with well-meaning and trusting people. Or voting for Ralph Nader.

In the dark, with no evident promise that the sun will ever rise, the Great Cringe sits on the edge of my bed, smiles a predator's smile, and says, "You are mine."

3

Some nights, I pick up one of R. D. Laing's books to help me understand my 3:00 a.m. self. R. D. Laing is a British psychiatrist, a dead one, except on moonless nights, when he comes back to life, sheeted and gibbering.

One of Laing's foundational ideas is that people create false selves to satisfy the demands of family and culture. But a false self and the story we tell about it divorce us not only from our real self, but also from the world.

Laing says that over time, a false self makes us crazy. Psychosis begins when we decide that our false self is our real self, and that the false world it lives in is the real one.

It happens no matter how smart you are. In fact, a side effect of being highly intelligent is that your false self and made-up world are less subject to breakdown than the false selves and made-up worlds of people less intelligent than you. If you're of genius-level intelligence, your false self is likely smarter than any other false self you encounter, which only looks like good news.

You seldom glimpse your false self when you look in the mirror, but you can see the false selves of other people. For a dismal example, the writer Ernest Hemingway spent his life constructing a writer's self and its accompanying story about a wounded guy who never complained. That's a hard story to live up to, no matter if you wrote *The Sun Also Rises* or not. When age and alcohol broke down Hemingway's self and story, there was nothing left to sustain his real self, and no real self left to sustain. Asking whether he was feeling guilty or sorry for himself is meaningless. His shotgun merely provided punctuation for a sentence already complete.

4

Losing faith in one's own story, false or not, is dangerous if not fatal. Fiction has the power to keep us alive, which is why we all practice creating it. Psychologists who treat abuse victims encounter screen memories in those victims, memories that shield someone from what they really experienced. These memories don't have to be false, not really. They just have to blot out the other memories, the ones that would destroy the self that remembers them.

My elementary school sins are screen memories. They're parts of a painful and sometimes funny story that is hiding something even harder to face, something that might destroy me if I let it come to consciousness. To put it simply: for all my life I've been a citizen of an America that knows what it's doing is unsustainable but does it anyway. That's easy enough to say and think about, especially in daylight. But somewhere in the crawl spaces of my brain, things are adding up to an understanding of what *unsustainable* means, and of how long we've got until it means it. That's what I'm not letting come to consciousness, not really.

5

R. D. Laing is concerned with individuals driven crazy by their construction of false selves. But what happens when an entire country also has a false self and a false story to back it up? For one thing, sanity will look a lot like craziness, even when you're sane. You have to be careful what you think in a country where for fifty years people have been telling themselves that they're richer than they are, that they can steal from generations unborn, that they stand for the cause of human freedom, that their economy can keep growing until it's bigger than the planet itself, and that they're mining and consuming inexhaustible resources according to their highest and best use.

That story is an elaborate psychosis. In reality, we spend more than we make. We torture detainees and steal children from their parents. We investigate the geology of countries before we invade them. We tolerate the manipulation of markets and tax codes that result in the working poor dying early, and the rich living longer but lacking the sort of purpose and imagination that would allow them to do something constructive with their freedom and power. We turn our gaze away from observable phenomena when they contradict projections of economic growth and technological triumph. We treat debt as wealth, which might be a sign of sanity, but only if you're holding the note.

Our truths rest on a foundation of magical thinking. The magic hasn't stopped yet, but it's fraying around the edges. The rabbit refuses to leave the hat. There's blood on the floor beneath the sawed-in-half woman. The Statue of Liberty vanishes from its pedestal and doesn't come back.

When Donald Trump came along, many people thought the creation of false selves had been raised to a high art. But his self and story have been falling apart since he came down his golden escalator to announce he was running for president, and that was possibly his strategy all along. He was not elected because people thought he was telling the truth, but because through his tissue of shoddy lies, people could begin to *discern the truth*, to see the dark, writhing shapes and hear the adenoidal grunts of the real. When your world begins to unravel, you start preferring the lies and liars you can see through to the ones you can't.

That's the durable, if perverse, contract between Trump and his base. A bleak survivalism has taken hold, even in that font of narrative called the Oval Office, even as the stock market and GNP go up and up.

6

Thank God I've finally quit sinning. That's the beginning of a new story, and a new self, and a new, reliable narrative character. Darrel might have written it.

Unfortunately, it's fiction. Darrel didn't write it, I did, and I lack his ability to ensure that everything fulfills the promise of its title. That's because my current narrative character is a white cisgender male, a retired writing and literature professor whose wife makes enough money editing over the Internet to occasionally take him to London theaters. He can buy gasoline and eat rib steaks at nice restaurants and spend long spring afternoons backcountry skiing. His conscience doesn't stop him from being or doing these things.

There are well-developed arguments that indicate such a life is a crime. They now and then come to mind, usually after happy and convivial dinners or when I look at my tracks from the bottom of a long powder run or while I'm ordering a glass of wine during intermission.

But repentance changes nothing. The Second Law of Thermodynamics could change something—a lot of things—and no doubt will, but for the moment it only wants me to dissipate the energy I've managed to accumulate. Most of the time I do just that.

I'm working on a blameless life with a lot less success. There are indications, now that the world is running short of fossil fuel, that divine justice and the Second Law are the same thing, but I've decided that regret should have its own Law of Thermodynamics, which states that in an isolated system like mine, guilt is a constant value that can neither be created nor destroyed. It attends to existence itself.

Forgiveness—and it's not clear from whom—will have to wait until the heat-death of the universe, and maybe longer. I spend time thinking about what will be inscribed in the granite of my tombstone, and whose eyes will read it, and if those eyes will be human or not.

He Meant Well is the current winning epitaph.

They Meant Well will serve for humanity's epitaph, too, although not everyone will agree that they did indeed mean well. A large percentage of humanity means no one well, if you look at the evidence.

7

When enough stories and their narrative characters turn out to be unreliable, false, or crazy, the social contract goes down.

A social contract is that combination of laws and customs that allows people to voluntarily trade their freedom for collective benefits, such as property rights, protection from uncontrolled violence, or health care for their children. In return for taxes they get courts and schools, a military, financial regulation, hospitals and roads and cities. If they're weak, they get sanctuary from the strong and powerful. If they're strong and powerful, they get limits enforced upon their appetites. You don't have to be Marcus Aurelius to know that such appetites, left to themselves, turn masters into slaves.

A strong social contract tends to create a hierarchy, one that generally endures until it ceases to deliver at least some benefits to everyone in the tribe, village, fan base, nation-state or, lately, civilization.

Social contracts that endure over centuries are the exception. If the bottom of any hierarchy consists of slaves or minimum-wage earners, it has a built-in instability. For the humans on the bottom, the cost is too much and the benefits too small.

Unless they want violent revolution or a brutal repressive stasis, the people at the top of the hierarchy have to pay attention to how many folks they put on the lowest level and how much energy they have to spend to keep them there.

If you're a slave in ancient Athens, your support for the social contract is more likely to be enforced at the point of a spear than by your appreciation of your city-state's advances in philosophy, art, and drama. If you're making minimum wage without health benefits in a twenty-first-century American franchise restaurant, you're keeping on keeping on because of a fear of homelessness, past-due college loans, or sick and starving children—rather than pride in your country's pioneering work in financial derivatives and progress in pharmaceuticals. If you're a poor artist in China, you produce art that supports the regime or your social credit score will go down, you'll lose your job, you'll get kicked out of your home, your work will be banned, and your niece won't be accepted into a university. In 2,500 years the point of the spear has become less visible, but it's still sharp enough.

Our country is currently debating whether the people on the bottom of the hierarchy should be allowed in the social contract at all. Lots of people are stumbling toward the bottom tiers. It's getting crowded down there, and there's a temptation to start kicking people out to make room for new arrivals.

Push them down a step in the hierarchy, and most people, even when they're lucky enough to retain some rights and privileges, will lose faith in the entire system. When enough people lose faith, the whole structure collapses. College loans don't get paid. Foreclosed houses fill up with people that law enforcement won't evict, because sheriff's deputies and police are living in foreclosed houses too. Nobody can afford oil at a price that would make drilling new wells worthwhile, even if they were sitting on lakes of the stuff, which they aren't.

There will be omens. Those in-laws who keep trying to sell you Amway products, those overly optimistic folks stuck with garages full of unsold household cleaner, nutritional supplements, and cosmetics, will start strutting around like they have real wealth, because they will. People on your street will cash out their 401(k)s in order to buy ammunition and camping gear, and they will research how to field dress your tabby cat. People will begin making papier-mâché piñatas out of dollar bills they find blowing down the sidewalk. At these points, you can assume that the social contract doesn't have much time left in your neighborhood.

Once it completely breaks down, what happens is agony to think about. Better—far better—to spend the dark hours remembering stupid things you did in grade school.

8

The stories that define life's parameters are called metanarratives. Metanarratives define the world and the purpose of living and how time works and what the self is and where we've been and where we're going. Without a metanarrative Darrel's parents would never have moved to a ski resort. Julie and I would never have moved back to Sawtooth Valley. George Bush would never have gone into Iraq.

The End of Civilization is a metanarrative. So are Utopia and Ecotopia, stories in which humans have learned to Live in Peace with Human Nature and with Their Planet. So is Laissez-Faire Capitalism, where The Market Will Make You Free, and Marxism, where History Will Make You Free, and Christianity, where Christ's Passion Has Washed Away Your Sins. Techno-futurists believe The Singularity Will Make You Free, Except You'll Have to Live in a Hard Drive.

A characteristic of metanarratives is their susceptibility to capitalization.

Metanarratives can look a little silly when presented this way, but if yours or mine malfunctions, the compass points of our existences disappear. R. D. Laing says schizophrenia—and its accompanying loss of self—occurs when a family's or culture's metanarrative contains so many contradictions that the individuals embedded in it stop believing in it.

We are currently surrounded by metanarratives that can no longer maintain anybody's self. If I had titled this chapter Free Energy from the Peaceful Atom, or Work Hard and Save Your Money and Prosper, I wouldn't expect you to put much faith in my thinking, much less believe anyone could base a self on it.

Instead, you would retreat into something less absurd, like The Illegal Hordes Won't Make It Through My Minefield and Steal My Krugerrands. Such a metanarrative preserves a self the same way you preserve peaches: first you kill all the bacteria, and then you seal yourself away from further contamination. You end up solitary and mad, but pristine.

R. D. Laing has a thought experiment that demonstrates how threatened we can get about the boundary between our self and the world. Think of drinking from a glass of water and, shortly thereafter, spitting in the same glass of water and drinking from it again.

Laing points out that sipping from a glass that we've spit into causes us great anxiety. Drinking from a glass we haven't spit into is the same mixing of water and saliva, but it doesn't bother us.

Our anxiety stems from an unexpected blend of what's inside and what's outside and the sudden consequent knowledge that the boundary of the self is arbitrary, permeable, and in danger of collapse. As a result, most of us have hard rules about what we willingly put into or take out of our mouths, nostrils, or any other orifice.

Substitute the borders of a country for the borders of the self and you can see how people can get so angry over foreigners crossing imaginary lines, even those foreigners who work their fields and serve them Big Macs and keep their houses clean and their lawns mowed.

9

The usual response when a metanarrative breaks is to go through an uncomfortable period of wondering if you have a self at all and then lie like crazy to get things back to where they were before the break, as when a fundamentalist Christian looks at a fossil and after some thought declares it an artifact of Satan.

It's hard to experience the breakdown of your metanarrative as anything but violence to your self and your family and your community, and such perceived violence begets more violence.

New metanarratives can be forged out of the scrap of broken ones. There's always a demagogue out there forging one from the basest, nastiest, most fearful and least sane parts of the human psyche. Scapegoats are invented. People whose existence represents a counter-narrative are lynched. Thoughts become crimes, and methods are invented to figure out what people are thinking.

The reason demagogues prosper is that the lies they offer are better than nothing, which is what the false self becomes in the absence of a good story. For people who have butchered their real selves to feed their false selves—that is, most of us—the choice is simple enough: buy into this cheap-ass fiction or wink into nonexistence.

10

Folie à deux is a psychiatric diagnosis that refers to a delusion shared by two persons. It's a helpful concept when you're making a case that reality is dependent on false selves and false narratives. Such craziness does not live in neurotransmitter dysfunction. It lives in the space between two or more people, sometimes in all the spaces between all the people in a country.

A case of *folie à deux* is a demonstration that personal observations do not always survive personal reality. If Frank notices all of Siberia bubbling methane, Dave says that it's normal climate oscillation. If Frank says tropical diseases are colonizing Canada, Dave blames South American refugees. If Frank says we're in the middle of a mass extinction, Dave says he doesn't see any extinct animals. If Frank quits his job and moves to a small farmstead in an isolated valley in Alaska where cabbages grow to the size of pumpkins, Dave sinks his life savings into the stock market and studies to become a broker.

Ultimately, Frank and Dave are headed for consensus. Dave will join Frank in Alaska for cabbage stew or Frank will join Dave's New York brokerage as a junior partner. They are bound together in ways they don't understand, ways that mostly have to do with Darrel wanting them to work things out.

But in spite of Darrel's good will and Frank and Dave's friendship, Frank's false self will fight to the death with Dave's false self. The false self that wins gets to make up the story for the false self that loses. That's the nature of Frank and Dave, and unfortunately that's the nature of humanity. It's another reason not to place your faith in history. Or even to place your faith in Frank and Dave stories, set in an imaginary world run by a benign and predictable god named Darrel.

Where is the self you started with in all this fakery and fiction? Often enough, it's extinct. But if yours is still alive, you can bring it back to health by going through life without preconceptions or paranoia. Buddhists say there's no such thing as a real self, but they suggest that reality can be found in chopping wood and carrying water, which is a gnomic way of saying that reality—and the self, if it exists—lives in doing and not in being, in focusing attention on the microcosm and not on the macrocosm, and in carefully observing the world in all its joy and tragedy, terror and wonder.

american history backward

It's easier to read in the mirror.

1

If you need a crystalline moment to show how far objective reality has fallen from favor in America, look back to the summer of 1990. That was when an American family received an out-of-court settlement from the Disney Corporation. The previous October, the family had been arrested—the whole family—in a gift shop at Disneyland. Their two-and-a-half-year-old daughter had been accused of shoplifting.

The family was taken to a Disneyland security office. After hours of involuntary incarceration, Disney auditors discovered that the piggy bank the little girl was hiding in her stroller really had been paid for. Not only that, but the gift shop had overcharged the family three dollars on their purchases.

Disney settled out of court, thinking it might be tough to find a jury unsympathetic to a two-and-a-half-year-old false-arrest victim overcharged for a piggy bank.

But the lawsuit was not concerned with false arrest. It was about loss of illusion.

As the family was taken to the security office, the couple's older daughter, four years old, observed a number of iconic Disney characters walking down a back alley with their giant grinning heads in their arms. Their real heads were human and were much too tiny for their bodies. Those big, friendly animals were really human beings being paid to walk around inside heavy and hot cartoon suits.

Back home after their ordeal, the family found themselves in a world unblessed by fantasy. The children began destroying their Disney toys. The parents tossed all Disney videos and Disney toys in the trash. The formerly cheerful and enthusiastic four-year-old refused to get out of bed or dress herself.

Children are realists. They pay attention to the world around them. Much psychotherapy focuses on those years from one to four, where our minds are inscribed with simple axioms: people close to you can or cannot be trusted, your family is a place where you're safe or where you're in constant danger, and you are or aren't able to apprehend what's real.

It's easy to understand how witnessing, say, a headless Goofy the Dog on the day your family got arrested for shoplifting could supply wrong answers to these questions.

Had the case gone to trial, we might have heard a psychiatrist bear witness to the awful damage reality can do to a child's mind. One can imagine a diagnosis of trauma-induced retail phobia, a condition rendering its victim into a permanent exile from souvenir gift shops, theme parks, malls, and Amazon websites.

2

It's sobering to realize that six of the last six American presidents have come from alcoholic families. The way such families make it through their dark nights of the soul is denial, which is to say, for example, that any pile of elephant shit on the TV room carpet is quickly identified as a footstool brought back from last year's vacation to Kenya, even when there was no Kenya and no vacation.

Consider:

Ronald Reagan's father was an alternately violent and sentimental alcoholic.

George H. W. Bush's father was an alcoholic.

Bill Clinton's stepfather was a violent alcoholic.

George W. Bush was an alcoholic. (I can't find much evidence that he was a violent alcoholic, but he was certainly a violent president.)

Barack Obama's father was an alcoholic.

Donald Trump's older brother was an alcoholic.

The politicians who rise to shape our national narrative are, of long necessity, adept at the magical thought and the happy lie. Their survival strategies have become the social-skill equivalent of misfolded brain proteins. Lies are told when it would be easier and less complicated to tell the truth. Illusion is preferred to seeing things as they are, even when illusion becomes nightmare.

Alcoholic families have disproportionately been training grounds for American politicians. From the time they were small, manipulative children, these people have known better than to look inward—in that direction lies madness, pain, and failure.

They know how to scapegoat. They crave the approval of others, something they seldom got while growing up. They are good at papering over broken relationships. If they seem emotionally numb, even in intimate moments, it's because numbness has allowed them to live with addicts.

Give them a chance, though, and they'll try to fix the world. The broken vase can be glued back together and put on a high shelf, even if it no longer holds water. The crumpled and torn photos can be hidden or burned, the smashed mirror above the mantel replaced with a pastoral painting, the police assured that everything is under control and nobody did anything wrong. An adult persona can be constructed when there's an addict in the house, but that persona hides an emotionally abandoned child still waiting for a birthday party that's happy, a dinner that doesn't end in rage. Truth-telling means contacting that child again, and too often that child has starved or gone mad. It's far better to impose a fictional stasis on the present.

Subjecting a politician to psychoanalysis isn't a job for the squeamish. Sometimes, under the carefully crafted image, it's only ashes, bones, shards, and tear-soaked, kapok-hemorrhaging, eyeless teddy bears.

And, of course, our politicians are addicts themselves. You push through the sex scandals and the corruption trials, through the fierce denials and eventual tears, to the realization that here are individuals all too representative of the people who elected them.

3

In 2004 George W. Bush's advisor Karl Rove might have told a *New York Times* reporter that America had become an empire, and that empires create their own realities. He might have meant that there was no longer any need for realists at the highest levels of American government. For that matter, he might have thought that at his level of government, there was no need for a real world at all.

Rove denies being the advisor in question. He calls it a weird quote and implies that he's not the kind of weird guy who would say it. The reporter conducted the interview under what might be called the Rules of Non-Attribution, which means an interviewee can be quoted but not identified.

High-administration officials are a mouthy bunch, but non-attribution makes it hard to pick them out of a crowd. Reporters have gone to jail to protect the anonymity of their sources, so if Rove says he didn't say that empires create their own reality, he can get away with it.

Rove implies the interview might not have occurred at all, which isn't a nice thing to do to a reporter. You don't accuse reporters of making up stories if you want them to retain credibility. You don't accuse presidential advisors or cabinet members or even presidents of making up stories for the same reason.

Nobody in journalism or government makes up stories if they don't want to contribute to a shifting, flexible reality where truth becomes solipsism, which proves Rove's point if he made it. It's not just that an empire creates its own reality. It creates its own psychosis.

Sanity becomes sedition. Deniability becomes the watchword of reality. Dissent—even the dissent of believing what you see—is suppressed, ridiculed, ignored, or institutionalized. These phenomena help to explain why almost everybody in power in America in 2003 supported invading Iraq to rid it of nonexistent weapons of mass destruction.

When an idea—no matter how warped—becomes the organizing principle of a personal or national consciousness, there is no experience that cannot be shaped to it, no bit of data that cannot be made to find its supporting role. Maybe that's the small truth that Karl Rove understood, if he said what he's rumored to have said.

Depending on your ability to spot subtle connections, you can realize you are not a desperate paycheck-to-paycheck American struggling to put food on the table, pay the rent, and get the kids through school. Instead, you're a long-lost Kardashian sister, stolen at birth from a hospital nursery. Or Elvis, pumped full of vitamins and the blood of eighteen-year-olds, finally ready for the comeback tour.

Not many Americans think they're either one these days. But they're not so devoted to childhood memories that they wouldn't be open to the possibility. After all, they're a people who have already chosen to forget vast chunks of their experience, especially when that experience suggests they've lost several wars in a row, that their lives require constant and expensive medication, and that they have hocked their grandchildren for oil.

It's hard to convince Americans to face a world where they're vulnerable and mortal and powerless in the face of events, when they can easily be someone else, someplace else.

4

At crucial times in American history, leaders surfaced who knew a real world did exist and it did need attention.

Lincoln, at great price, stopped the commodification of human beings. Teddy Roosevelt stopped a corporate takeover of the nation, and the sale of the remaining wild lands in the American West. Franklin Roosevelt stopped our homegrown fascists, and then the Nazis and the Imperial Japanese, who were commodifying people in such brutal ways that it couldn't be disguised as anything but murder.

These three were great full-time presidents because they were at least part-time realists.

After the Second World War, realism was in vogue for a while, no doubt helped along by the realities of the Nazi Holocaust as well as the smaller holocausts of Hiroshima, Nagasaki, and Dresden.

American realism's finest hour occurred in 1948, when

advisor George F. Kennan pointed out to President Truman that America had 50 percent of the world's wealth but only 6.3 percent of its population, and that the country needed to devise a foreign policy to keep things that way.

Kennan said the United States of America should construct alliances and understandings with the elites of lesser nations that would keep them elite while allowing America to maintain its percentage of the world's property. Such alliances and understandings—the levers of empire—were necessary to counter the resentment that our wealth would inspire in the rest of the world.

Demonstrating a capacity for a subtle *realpolitik* that Bismarck might have envied, Kennan suggested we could remain a beacon of liberty and democracy while using military and economic power to stay rich.

Kennan's most powerful idea was the physical, political, and economic containment of the Soviet Union. He wrote that communist idealism wouldn't survive its collision with a material-rich America. Over generations the Soviet Union's exceptionalist, democratic, rights-of-man fantasy would fall to the greed, laziness, corruption, and general incompetence of the people who ran it.

You can argue that Kennan's narrative of the Soviet system and its future prevented nuclear war between the United States and the Soviet Union. You can argue that any sacrifice of ideals and treasure was worth that non-outcome, even if the policy of containment did give rise to the Shah of Iran, Henry Kissinger, Vietnam, the Cambodian genocide, various coups and proxy wars in Africa and Latin America, and the Iraq and Afghanistan wars and their ugly sequels.

Kennan died in 2005 at 101. He had seen realism destroyed by Ronald Reagan's Morning in America, but he was still a few years short of witnessing his country's fall to the greed, laziness, corruption, and general incompetence of the people who ran it.

5

Philosophers of science say the scientific method is the best way the human mind has ever devised to apprehend reality.

God help us.

Hard data can show that the planet Venus has a greenhouse effect, too, and that ten years of having rib steak and ice cream for dinner will cause a rise in cardiovascular disease in a population of stressed, paranoid, and subliminally angry mid-management males. It can show that DNA is damaged by the ionizing radiation from a reactor meltdown, and that the cheaply tapped deposits of fossil fuels are gone. It can show that many huge, slow, and tasty animals disappeared from Australia and the Americas the same time human beings arrived.

But you can't be certain that greenhouse-gas emissions from industrial civilization will result in a runaway greenhouse effect that will turn the earth and Venus into identical planets. You can't be sure that industrial civilization will decline in proportion to a shortfall of fossil fuels, or that burning those fossil fuels will cause lethal climate change, or that brooding male middle-managers who want to avoid a heart attack should become vegetarian Buddhists. You can't say that hunter-gatherers have caused extinctions, even when Clovis points are found in the bones of wooly mammoths.

Counter-narratives exist for all these assertions:

More carbon dioxide will transform the earth into a pleasantly warmer green Eden, one where sequoias return to Ellesmere Island. Abiotic oil, formed deep within the earth, will constantly replenish depleted oil wells.

Real men eat beef, barbequed if not raw, and whatever else they can afford. They never admit to vulnerability, not even to their cardiologists, and their deaths will be somebody else's problem.

When people first walked the earth, they lived in harmony with charismatic megafauna, and they would still if they had been left alone.

The scientific method may be the best method of apprehending reality the human mind has ever devised. It's not clear, however, that the human mind can apprehend the scientific method.

Data and narrative have ceased to have any connection. In a scientific arena of any magnitude—it's hard to imagine a scientific arena so small that a dozen quark-sized angels can't be comfortably clubbing each other to death in it—any hypothesis generates skeptical opposition. A flurry of alternate hypotheses generates, in turn, a deep policy inertia.

A sample hypothesis: you can know things through the scientific method, but you can't use the scientific method to think your way out of an embedded cultural narrative, even when that cultural narrative looks like a lie.

6

At Disneyland, all the employees not in cartoon suits are required to smile and keep smiling, upon pain of dismissal. It's a logical rule at an institution that gives children and accompanying adults respite from a place where the cartoon characters are the Four Horsemen of the Apocalypse, where Tomorrowland is a place where poor old people steal cat food from employed people's cats, where the bad toys have all the batteries, and where the rides are crawling commutes to and from mind-numbing jobs. Goofy the Dog's giant head is a latex illusion, but it's an illusion we accept with relief.

But we ignore the person required to maintain that illusion. Some guy's *in* there, carrying forty-seven pounds of rubber and fiberglass and nylon, worrying that after a decade of wandering around Disneyland and having his picture taken with three-year-olds, he'll *be* Goofy, and he'll forget the Magic Kingdom even has an exit. When Mickey and Minnie and Donald crowd around and try to take his Goofy suit off, he'll show his teeth and growl.

Anyone watching the Federal Reserve Chair's body language as he reports the latest economic news, or watching House Judiciary Committee hearings on C-SPAN, or watching a political rally on Fox News—anyone who doesn't realize the people onscreen are all trapped and sweating inside Goofy suits—hasn't been paying attention.

7

In writing classes, where I could cover a wide range of topics without violating the syllabus, I used to end semesters by telling young Americans of good will and optimism not to have kids. "Buy a Bentley instead," I'd say. "It's cheaper. While gasoline is still available, you can drive it to Disneyland. After that, you can live in it."

My words didn't go over well with an audience planning to live like their parents had. They anticipated children, homes, education, and food. Football. Girl Scouts. Dogs. Horses.

In the face of frowns or a studied disinterest, I kept going.

"I know it's none of my business whether you have kids or not," I said, with a disarming smile. "But they make it hard to vacation in Tuscany or pay off education loans. Forget about getting a mortgage. Forget about nice restaurants, where kids make the help nervous anyway.

"Besides, because world population has already exceeded sustainable resources, they'll die of disease, violence, or starvation. Either that or become addicts who will trade your granddaughters for a bottle of Oxycontin.

"Don't leave," I said. "This is for your own good."

I was asking them to forgo the Magic Kingdom for an America where tentacled darkness crawls inside mouths that utter nothing but applause lines. It's a hard sell.

A scientist friend says this: "Those of us with children and grandchildren cannot go there."

8

When did America's founding Anglos exile themselves from what F. Scott Fitzgerald, in the closing pages of *The Great Gatsby*, calls "the fresh, green breast of the new world?" When did they reject the last place "commensurate to [their] capacity for wonder" and choose to live instead among the waste products of their imaginations?

From nearly the beginning, as far as I can tell. The idealistic language of the Declaration of Independence, the preamble to the American Constitution, and the Constitution itself came out of an established utopian tradition—where the world of the real is transformed into the island of the ideal—in British fiction.

Two examples come immediately to mind: *Utopia* and *Gulliver's Travels*. The more erudite among the Founding Fathers had likely encountered *Utopia*, a social-engineering tract thinly disguised as a travelogue, in their studies of Renaissance political philosophy.

Utopia was written in 1516 by Henry VIII's troublesome priest, Thomas More. It mapped the size and shape of the ideal island state and the rules that made it work. Like a lot of ideal states, More's depended on slaves to do its hard or unpleasant labor. Its true citizens were expected to devote their leisure to philosophy or worship.

Most of the Founders also would have been familiar with the Irish satirist Jonathan Swift. Swift's 1726 fictional travelogue, *Gulliver's Travels*, described various nations, insulated by oceans or floating in the sky, that had developed cultures different from those of Europe. Swift's islands had their faults— chief among them residents who sported a glossy combination of lofty pretense and base desire—but their separation from the known world made them perfect arenas for governments based on ideas.

Even without these influences, the Founders would have been utopian thinkers. They were the new owners of a huge, resource-rich, and recently depopulated continent, one that was in essence an island.

When you're a successful revolutionary you can map out any future, no matter how much at odds with the present, proclaim it to be the future, and then construct laws and institutions to fit. Once a fiction has been acted upon, it gains a legitimacy that can substitute for truth.

Even those Founders who didn't see themselves as writing on the blank parchment of a rich, unclaimed continent, who knew that it would in fact take a genocide to scrape that parchment clean, didn't insist that such cleansing be brought to the attention of their more idealistic compatriots.

To put it another way: Thomas Jefferson was a brilliant theoretician and a superb writer, but he used his skills to write exceptionalist rights-of-man fantasy that his slaves wouldn't have found remotely applicable to their lives.

But that isn't the point. Jefferson's freedom to do what he wanted—and we know he was a man of large and diverse appetites—had once been infringed upon by King George III, a parliament that considered Americans rude bumpkins, and laws that kept the colonies as sources of raw material rather than of finished goods. His authorship of the Declaration of Independence made it all go away. Jefferson's literary resentment toward an oppressive reality became a feature of the nation he founded. It wouldn't be the last time the country witnessed fiction turn into nonfiction.

9

The Founders drew up an all-too-human map for a divine territory, and then they followed their map. Students of American history have noted a chronic, if futile, American tendency to counter spiritual emptiness by making material wealth into a religion. While America may have been founded as a democracy, it was also a theocracy dedicated to the fervent worship of Mammon, the insatiable god of money.

Foreign visitors to the new republic, notably de Tocqueville, commented on the American obsession with becoming rich. De Tocqueville saw not only the love of money but the bad craziness that the love of money gave rise to: the commodification of everybody and everything.

It *is* bad craziness. If you commodify a forest of oak trees or a herd of buffalo or a ship's hold of people, you have incorporated that forest and herd and those people into a vast imaginary system of ledger sheets and tax receipts and market futures. What remains of the real are stump farms or vast piles of bloody bones or the graves of slaves.

In recent decades giant dairy farms have sprung up a hundred miles south of Sawtooth Valley. They have replaced small family farms as the backbone of Idaho agriculture, and they run like large factories. The production of dairy products at that scale produces a stinking miasma that oozes over the landscape, although it hasn't oozed this far north yet. Farther south, whether you breathe through your mouth or nose depends on the direction of the wind, unless of course you're surrounded by dairies, in which case you're a full-time mouth-breather.

But follow Mammon, and you'll identify the odor of a giant dairy as the smell of money, repurposing in the process one of your more important senses. It's a bad idea to repurpose that particular sense, since its job is to discern between the sustaining and the lethal. Dairies, like the rest of industrial civilization, seem to embody both.

A dangerous resonance exists between utopian thinking and the love of money. You may find that your ability to convert your sense of smell into dollars increases with the distance you live from the dairy.

To the extent you can buy reality off—that you can use money to buy a house tens of miles upwind of the dairy, for example—you can say that reality is for people who lack money.

10

Recent research indicates that your brain structure changes when you spend five or six hours a day playing video games or surfing the Internet. Some cortical regions atrophy and other regions expand. Your attention span, your relations with other people, your need for stimulation, and your language usage all mutate. To paraphrase Heisenberg, it would take a resilient universe to stay stable in the face of such changes in the observer.

A thought experiment: envision the computer screen you stare at as the narrow part of an hourglass. That screen transmits the myriad bits of the Internet to your brain, which creates an electrochemical simulacrum of itself, in among the folds of the wetware.

A symmetry emerges between two realities, one that gives credence to the philosophers who hold that reality only exists in the electrical charges zipping from neuron to neuron in our skulls. Their position supports complacency in the face of external developments like multi-decade droughts in the Midwest, drone wars in the Mideast, or the tundra that covers Siberia and northern Canada suddenly generating enormous amounts of methane.

These are only problems in the wetware. No wetware, no problem. No reality, for that matter.

Most people reject this sort of problem solving. But it's true that the wetware has created the world of artifice and algorithms we live in, and when I say there's a real world, that's what I'm talking about. Like it or not, we are living in the America our ideas have created.

For the moment we can live in it. But for the moment, imagine what reality-as-usual might give birth to: aside from a radically different climate and the occasional nuclear accident, the Gross National Product will continue its rise, fueled by a boom in green technology and beach-cottage replacement.

There will be stunning advances in digital entertainment, gene-editing miracles, electric cars, ever more precise and effective weapons—collateral damage and opposition to Empire may end simultaneously—and ever more franchise restaurants.

Wilderness areas will finally be assigned a cultural and economic value when they are reconstructed far above sea level, inside insulated and cooled structures. Population growth will be helped along by genetically improved wheat and rice and algae-generated diesel. Cities will become great walled hives.

Efficiencies in resource use and communication will allow economies to prosper in the face of shrinking energy and materials. Longevity drugs will allow Social Security recipients to return to work as centenarians. A gentle inflation will gradually erase all long-term debt.

Or not. Maybe we'll end up in an America resembling George F. Kennan's nightmare, a moonscaped radioactive desert where the survivors are confined to caves and ruins and drink ash-fouled water and don't look too closely at the meat they're eating, and knowledge and technology diminish with each burned book and broken machine and dead battery.

It's a measure of human adaptability that should the results of nuclear war be slower—that climate change and economic collapse spread them over eighty years—people will go about their lives without much awareness that their yesterdays were different than their todays.

They may remember short visits to the outside. It will not have been home to them. Home will be the dark basement of an abandoned building when it isn't a half-flooded subway tunnel, but it will have its comforts, survival among them.

Lifespans will shorten. The melted remains of nuclear power plants will ionize chromosomes, but not so much that people won't have the occasional normal kid, and those children will have the occasional normal kid.

Even were we to project our darkest trends forward to that day when the last band of Americans is fighting the last band of cockroaches for the last cache of civil-defense crackers, I'd put my money on the Americans, who have utopia in their makeup.

I'd make a side bet that cockroaches end up a domesticated food source.

One last wager: I'd bet that the children of that last band, wandering with cockroach breath through the dark corridors of a ruined city, will look up through holes in concrete, will see the unshielded metallic glint of the dawn. They will greet the new day with awe. They will wonder at the miracle of existence.

vietnam as simulacrum

Tourism is virtual reality for baby boomers.

1

In the second decade of the twenty-first century, it's still possible to buy two round-trip plane tickets from Idaho to Vietnam for two thousand dollars. Once there, it's cheaper than staying home. A clean hotel room with a shower and toilet costs two people fifteen to twenty-five dollars and includes breakfast. Lunch can be locally grown fruit. It's hard to eat a dollar's worth. A lavish dinner for two—curry, or a seafood hot-pot, or braised pork ribs, or prawns in tamarind sauce—costs ten dollars. Beer is a dollar a bottle and good. Wine is expensive and not so good.

If you're a rich American tourist, you can go into the tall hotels and take elevators to rooftop restaurants where the menu prices are in dollars, the tables have bouquets, and the chairs wear tablecloths. But even with Vietnamese inflation running at 12 percent or so, being a rich American tourist in Vietnam isn't nearly as costly as being one in Venice or Barcelona or London.

If you are a Vietnamese farmer, it's different. In the second decade of the twenty-first century, it can be hard to pay for food and fuel. Of course, the first decade was worse. In 2009 inflation was 24 percent, which drove lots of farmers' children off the land and into the cities.

The reason for this inflation has been an infusion of foreign capital, some brought in by tourists, but most brought in by people building infrastructure for tourists. Earlier rounds of inflation came with the clothing and electronics factories that were built when the Vietnamese government offered up its human resources to international capitalism.

The government doesn't call it capitalism. They call it enhanced communism, and sure enough, the government takes an enhanced and sometimes informal cut from the new factory builders and the new factory workers and the construction companies and anyone else who wants to invest in Vietnam.

But tourism is regarded as the real cash cow, now and in the future. Neighboring Thailand has made an art form of tourism, building whole resort cities on islands that once held only rubber plantations and fishing villages.

The Vietnamese are following Thailand's example. They, too, want eight-hundred-dollar hotel rooms and sex tourists and people who will buy Armani suits from people not named Armani. They ignore signs that Thailand's tourist industry has been overbuilt, with half-empty hotels lining its beaches even before the crash of 2008.

People hoping to get in on the ground floor of the Next Best Place are offering money and credit, and the government admits anyone with the price of admission. There is reason for their optimism. Vietnam is as beautiful as Thailand, but its beaches aren't as crowded with tourists. That's a good thing, at least in the eyes of tourists, who can be a self-loathing species.

But not all of the tourists in Vietnam are looking for the perfect deserted beach, the most primitive trek, or the best curry dish in the world. Not all of them are looking for low-priced art or antiques. Not all of them are looking to lie drunk on a sun-drenched beach chair for two weeks. Some of them are looking for their youth, and in Vietnam, some of them can pinpoint the spot where they saw it last.

2

I didn't take the first chance I had to go to Vietnam. That was in May of 1968, when I graduated from high school. Some of my classmates had joined the Marines that spring, and what their high school commencement commenced was boot camp.

I went to college instead. With a student deferment, I didn't have to worry about going to war until I graduated or had a semester below a C average. But midway through my junior year, Congress instituted a draft lottery. Someone had noticed that black kids were going to war and white kids were going to school.

The night of the lottery, my college roommate and I purchased a six-pack of Rolling Rock, a bag of Doritos, and two cans of bean dip.

Our lives were tied to the numbers that were picked for us, but we didn't understand that. We each opened a beer, scooped up gobs of bean dip with our Doritos, and turned on the radio. The lottery started. My roommate's draft number was two. The party was over.

My roommate enlisted rather than be drafted into the infantry, and he ended up going to language school and learning Japanese. He spent his war on Okinawa, eavesdropping on Japanese military communications. Once out of the Army, he became an auto mechanic in Philadelphia, probably the only one capable of reading Toyota shop manuals in their original language.

My own number was 117. People with that same number

did get drafted, but as far as my local Selective Service Board was concerned, it was high enough for them to let me be. It's possible that my board chose to honor deferments that had ceased to exist. It's possible, too, that someone else was drafted in my place. There was not much transparency, or even consistency, in draft-board decisions toward the end of the war.

So Vietnam didn't teach me Japanese, or Vietnamese either. But it shaped who I became. The concept and execution of the war gave me a deep distrust of the powerful and inept old men of my government. It gave the lie to my plans to go to law school, become wealthy, live in a gated subdivision, learn to play golf, and end up powerful and inept.

I couldn't articulate those thoughts at eighteen. I did know that Vietnam had pushed my life out of its projected path into one deeply suspicious of power and wealth. Some latent gene had been activated. It was like suddenly discovering that you were adopted, and that your real parents were Vietnamese. Who knew?

3

In the second decade of the twenty-first century, Julie and I fly into Saigon from Boise, Idaho. It's a twenty-three-hour trip. We land at two-thirty in the morning. We are jet-lagged and confused.

Right away, we are ripped off in a taxi scam. It costs us thirty-five dollars to be delivered to the wrong hotel. It would have cost us ten to be delivered to the right one, had we accepted our hotel's offer of an airport pickup. It's our first encounter with Vietnamese economic policy and our own vulnerability to it. It will remain in our minds during all subsequent transactions in Vietnam.

The good news is that over the next two months we will save far more than the twenty-five dollars we lost to the taxi-scammer. Scam victims turn into hard bargainers.

We cease being good-willed and uncritical travelers, free with our dollars and excited about guided tours and shipping local souvenirs home to friends and family. Instead we look for the next person who might rip us off. We purchase nothing that isn't absolutely essential to our trip. We become expert in the averted gaze, the quick shake of the head, the memorized guidebook phrase in Vietnamese that means—variously modified by body language—"No-thank-you-not-interested-leave-us-alone-go-away-you're-violating-my-Western-concept-of-personal-space."

I take the lead in this matter, refusing treks and motorcycle taxi rides to what are always deemed the best hotels in town. "We're not rich American tourists," I say to anyone who approaches us speaking English. "We're poor American tourists."

But there is no way to translate "poor American tourist" into Vietnamese. Americans get to Vietnam on jet planes. And these days, they can leave Vietnam when they want, starting the process by tapping their smart phones. They consume impossibly huge portions of food in impossibly expensive restaurants. They make a show of praying in Buddhist temples, even when they're not Buddhist. They're on a permanent vacation from hard choices, insulated from discomfort or consequence by cards that cause money to vomit from ATM machines.

When a poll was taken of young people in Southeast Asia, asking them what they most desired in life, a majority said an ATM card.

We walk instead of ride around Saigon, watching and taking photos but disturbing as little as possible, taking nothing, like visitors careful to stay on a boardwalk in a national park. We do not take a tour. For reasons of horror and claustrophobia, we do not visit the Cu Chi tunnels—the nearby hiding place of an entire Viet Cong battalion during the war—even though they've been enlarged to accommodate Western bodies. We do not visit Saigon's red-light district, which, like Bangkok's, has become a tourist attraction.

Guidebook in hand, we walk around our crowded neighborhood. We visit the Museum of Fine Arts and the war rooms under the presidential palace of the Republic of South Vietnam. We find some good restaurants and, once, an air-conditioned coffee shop where the logos, counter, tables, chairs, and prices are all modeled on Starbucks. We tour Chinese Buddhist temples, but we do not pray in them.

Saigon is crowded with seven or eight or nine million people, depending on how far out from the city center you designate the city limits. Motorcycles are the usual form of transportation. Most intersections lack traffic lights. Five or six streams of traffic, fifty motorcycles wide, move through each other without as many collisions as you'd expect. The decibel level is in the hearing-damage range.

Our hotel is comfortable and in a neighborhood of restaurants and shops, but we leave after three days.

The reason? The size of Saigon, its traffic, its touts, its noise, the professional beggars displaying baskets of rented Agent-Orange-mutated children, the warnings in our guidebook about thieves on motorcycles dragging female tourists down the street by their purses until one or the other lets go. We take a minibus south through the flat maze of the Mekong Delta and, after a couple of nights in brusque government-run hotels, get on a ferry that takes us to Vietnam's southernmost territory, the island of Phu Quoc.

4

Life on Phu Quoc: Up at dawn, watch the sunrise off the balcony. Walk down to the restaurant, have a coffee, have another coffee. Walk a mile along the beach or until you pass a hundred thousand lost flip-flops, whichever comes first. Walk back. Have lunch. Start a new book, found in your hotel's exchange library. Feed the tan. Swim in the crashing surf. Have a beer. Have dinner. Finish the new book.

Watch the evening thunderstorm march across the water on legs of lightning. When the rain hits, head for the suite for the night. Go to sleep to thunder. Dream dreams unstained by thoughts of who did what to whom.

Rinse. Repeat.

We stay at a small boutique hotel on a secluded southern beach of the island. Our suite is all teak and marble and chrome and beveled glass. But there is no electricity after 10:00 p.m. No television anytime. No hot water, even though our bathroom has a Jacuzzi tub inset into its marble surfaces. Not much water pressure, either. It would take all day to fill the tub. But the shower dribbles enough cool water to wash off the salt after a day at the beach.

Julie and I don't normally stay at boutique hotels, but most of the planned rooms of our hotel weren't supposed to be boutique. It was supposed to be much larger, with fifteen or twenty backpacker's bungalows out behind the four luxury suites of the hotel building. Our suite, I decide, is the first owner's intended residence, although it looks as if the first owner stopped owning it years ago.

We are alone, save for one other couple, who keep to themselves. The common areas, the kitchen, the restaurant, and the gift shop are large and lonely. They were built for the crowds that were to come with Phase II.

Phase II is nowhere to be seen. Work has yet to start on the bungalows, or on a good water system, or on the power lines to run twenty air-conditioning units. Meanwhile, Phase I looks like entropy is getting the better of it, despite the efforts of a small army of landscapers, beach attendants, waitresses, and bartenders.

From the balcony I see peeling paint and the balding thatch of aging beach umbrellas. The hotel's two Jet Skis sit rusting in a litter-filled building that has hand-crafted rock walls and Gothic windows. The master plan must have included a chapel.

The crippled luxury and smoldering hope of our hotel fit our budget. Our biggest objection to the place is that at dinner, the stereo plays Abba's greatest hits when it isn't playing soft instrumentals of Abba's greatest hits.

But the food is good. The bartender is attentive and generous. In the mornings expert massages are available for a few dollars on the beach.

Long walks along the coastline cost time, sunscreen, and the purchase of a picnic lunch and bottled water from the kitchen. A climb over the headlands on either side of our beach reveals more beaches and more shoals of plastic, and now and then a single standing wall of a collapsed house, a remnant of the time before the war.

5

At the end of World War II, the population of Vietnam was less than twenty-five million. Now it's over ninety-seven million, in spite of war-related losses that approached five million. Population density is 814 people per square mile, more than twice that of China. Over 70 percent of present-day Vietnamese were not born when the Vietnam War ended in 1975.

It's a country of young and hopeful people, and there's no apparent worry among them that they will ever run out of resources to exploit or markets to sell to. But Julie and I, wandering around, see inflation-impoverished old people, unemployed young ones, a substantial part of the workforce selling lottery tickets, and tons of new plastic crap in the markets on its way to becoming the tons of old plastic crap that mark the tide lines of every beach we visit.

In the cities you pass rows of shops, all well-stocked with goods and empty of customers. Too often a row of shops all sell the same merchandise: T-shirts, religious trinkets, sunscreen, watches, liquor, umbrellas, purses, ballpoint pens, baseball caps, detergent.

In beach towns you can spot new hotels by the construction cranes. The buildings are skeletal monsters with hundreds of rooms, half-completed but open for business just as soon as a room is ready. Guests walk through unfinished hallways to swimming pools and dining rooms. On nearby streets restaurants park children on the sidewalk, and it's not uncommon to have tiny smiling girls thrust menus under your nose five or six times in a single block. Some variation of this transaction—the offer followed by the refusal, a quick shake of the head and avoidance of eye contact unless hunger has just hit—characterizes much tourist activity in Vietnam.

Every year the new Vietnamese economy grows an official 7 percent, and that growth is seen as proof that things will get better and better, until everyone has an ATM card.

Boosters of capitalism tout its capacity for creative destruction, but more than once in Vietnam I had the thought that what was being destroyed was a nation's capacity for empathy and altruism.

It's not just tourists who have come to be seen as units of profit rather than as people. The Vietnamese, especially the young adults, compete with each other on a life-and-death basis. The prize? Something that looks suspiciously like the American dream—as envisioned by a paycheck loan company's marketing department.

6

We make a temporary incursion into Cambodia.

Kampot.

It's a small, lazy town on an estuary that leads to the Gulf of Thailand. The food is different from Vietnam—spicier, less vegetarian, cheaper, every bit as good. Our hotel is clean and new. A small population of English-speaking expatriates is happy to recount tales of family estrangement for the price of a beer.

A few blocks from our hotel, the Honey Bar, a dark-doorwayed saloon whose outside sign features a dissipated Pooh Bear hoisting a beer mug, is for sale for five thousand dollars. The price includes the girls who work there.

Phnom Penh.

Cambodia's capital. The burden of its history is too much for us. We leave as quickly as we can, distressed by the taxi drivers' incessant cries: "Killing Fields? You want to go to Killing Fields?" That, and our discovery that our hotel has been built on the site of one of the Khmer Rouge's slaughterhouses.

Siem Reap.

A tourist city, now, expanded to serve the millions of tourists who visit Angkor Wat. A thousand years ago Angkor was the biggest city in the world, ten miles on a side, home to a million people. It shows the grotesque scale of our own time that two to three times that many were killed by the Khmer Rouge alone.

We visit the ruins on three consecutive days and find nothing among their vined temples and broken towers to indicate that having the biggest city in the world does a civilization much good in the long run.

In Kampot we had encountered a down-at-his-heels Australian running a small-time tour business with his Cambodian in-laws. He explained for us the pathologically laid-back attitude of Cambodians: "Most of them had their whole families killed by the Khmer Rouge. They live with no sense of the future."

7

Notes on Hanoi, which is a short flight and a world away from Cambodia.

It is not laid-back. It's the capital of the people who won the war. What they won is a huge and diverse and officially unified nation, although Hanoi contains plenty of evidence that deep divisions remain between rich and poor, young and old, north and south, mountain and lowland, ethnic Chinese and ethnic Vietnamese.

Also between communists and the people. Communism still has a religious heft in Hanoi. Party members are the high priests of that religion, even as capitalism pays the bills. A few of the self-sacrificing heroes of 1975 are still in power, and younger middle-aged bureaucrats still pay lip service to the worldwide struggle against imperialism.

A still younger generation of communists is composed of a familiar international breed: intelligent but unimaginative young people who do all the right things in high school and university to twist their way into the existing power structure. Once there, they display a commendable respect for enforcing rules, following procedures, and advancing their careers. But like the generation before them, they have little ideological backbone when it comes to keeping their fingers out of the cookie jar, and Vietnam's corruption index matches that of Ethiopia, Mongolia, and Tanzania.

A local magazine survey of Hanoi residents reveals that what Hanoians want most in life is not an ATM card. They want a car. This, in spite of the fact that if everybody in Hanoi who wants a car gets one, there would be no room—none—on the already gridlocked streets. There won't be enough fuel to go around, either. Or clean air. Or undamaged pedestrians.

The national government has been notably successful in housing the homeless and the dispossessed, although much of that housing has come at the expense of agriculture, cultural monuments such as temples and cemeteries, and the geography itself. Much of Vietnam is made up of limestone mountains, and those mountains are gradually being ground into powder. Giant cement factories exist in every large town, community epicenters of mercury pollution and brown coal smoke. A good portion of the country's labor is used to mix the product of those factories with water and gravel and pour it into forms. Other than the giant hotels being built for tourists, there are a limited number of forms: one for family housing, one for multi-family housing, one or two for small hotels and commercial buildings. Different colored ceramic facades distinguish one building from another.

Countless numbers of these five- to ten-story buildings are being built within Hanoi and down the coast. There are vast towns in Vietnam that have the feel and the look of American suburbs, except for the fact that they're taller and made of concrete and they don't have any lawns.

Someday, you think, there will be no mountains left in the country. In their place will be a vast glazed hive, a labyrinth a thousand miles long, with caste-specific cells for former farmers, bankrupt shopkeepers, old soldiers, disillusioned party members, and low-budget tourists.

8

We arrive in Nha Trang, the tourist city just up the coast from Cam Ranh Bay. A week before we arrive, an international tourist organization has listed Nha Trang as one of the ten worst beach towns in the world. We don't know that when we check into the Ha Van hotel, where friendly people usher us to a nice twenty-dollar room that comes with the best breakfast we'll have in Vietnam. We don't know that when we discover the Louisiana Brew House, across the shore highway from the Ha Van, where you can sit by the pool all morning in eighty-degree sunshine, drinking good Czech beer and reading the cold parts of *Dr. Zhivago*, until it's time to eat lunch at poolside or in the attached restaurant. We don't know that when we walk through the town's beachfront sculpture garden, or when we visit its Cham Dynasty towers—thousand-year-old ruins that have been restored on a hill at the north end of town. We especially don't know that when, on the way back from the towers, we find an inexpensive Indian restaurant on a narrow backstreet right across from an ATM.

Nha Trang is the most touristed place we visit in Vietnam, but we've become hardened to the beggars and street hawkers and sidewalk touts, and they have learned to read the signs of that hardening, and they leave us alone. Nha Trang has a forest of high-rise hotels, but some of them are dark and empty even though the weather is good and lots of foreigners walk the streets. A half-dozen more high-rise skeletons are going up, powered skyward by some heliotropic twitch of international capital.

If you dine upstairs at the Indian restaurant, you look across the street to a clothing factory, where the teenaged workers get ready for bed right next to their sewing machines. They look out at you with eyes a hundred years old. They see you looking back at them, and you both realize how unbridgeable the gap is between you, how improbable for each is the gaze of the other. The blinds come down with a snap. You go back to your beer and lamb vindaloo.

These things are hardly the stuff of ten-worst lists. Perhaps the sin that Nha Trang has committed is sprawling into a miles-long international party, a twenty-story carnival of shopping, eating, and drinking on a gorgeous white-sand half-moon beach. It doesn't help that the beach lies between two fog-topped mountain headlands and faces a soft-blue bay full of dark-green islands. Like many of the world's inhumanly beautiful places, this one has been reduced to the limits of human imagination by its tourist industry.

There is a kind of headless chicken momentum to Nha Trang, even when it's clear that much more success as a tourist attraction will kill what was the attraction in the first place. But even so, Nha Trang is in less danger of reaching that point than Koh Samui or Pattaya in Thailand, or even Phu Quoc. Its boom comes at the wrong moment in history.

We want to go back in another ten years. We'd like another week around the pool at the Louisiana Brew House. We'd like to see what becomes of a place built on middle-class purchases of airline tickets once the middle class has ceased to exist.

9

In the mountain town of Dalat, home to Vietnam's wine industry, a university, a replica of the Eiffel Tower, an astonishing botanical garden, and the extravagant summer palace of

Vietnam's last emperor, we strike up a conversation with our waiter in the restaurant across the street from our hotel.

He speaks good English and acts happy to see us. He's twenty-one years old and goes to Dalat University. He grew up on his parents' coffee farm. His name is Kong, he says, like King Kong. He flexes his muscles and laughs.

He asks us where we're from, and we say America and ask where he's from, and he says from his mother. It's a joke we've heard before in Vietnam. We ask where his mother's from, and he says his parents live north of Dalat. He doesn't see them often. They cannot leave their coffee farm. When Kong isn't working as a waiter, he needs to study.

Kong wants to meet us for coffee in the morning. He has some questions he wants to ask us, and we reluctantly agree. I tell Julie that if he tries to sell us something or sign us up for a trek, I'm out the door. But Kong wants information, not money.

"How can I get rich?" he asks, even before the coffee comes.

I'm not the person to ask, I tell him. I revert to an old cultural narrative and tell him to work hard, save his money, and do everything he can to stay out of debt.

"I am already doing that," he says.

I say, "It doesn't always work. Not everyone who follows the rules gets rich. Besides, it's a game where the winners lose. Some money is good, but you can have too much. It can make you into its own image."

"Interesting," he says, by which he means, "Bullshit."

His English isn't so good that I can tell him that America has lost more than just the war and there's no need to adopt our values.

I ask him about his family's farm, and he says it's on a steep hillside where each coffee plant has to be watered by hand in the dry season. He has one brother and three sisters. His brother will run the farm. His sisters will be married to other farmers. He is the oldest son, and for that reason he was chosen to go to university. I decide that when he's asking about getting rich, he's asking about freeing his parents from a life of hard labor. To a tourist who's been waiting for the next taxi scam for six weeks, sudden feelings of empathy come as a shock.

Kong asks how old I am. I tell him. He says his parents are younger than me but they look older. Then he says that he would like to own a car someday, when he's a hotel manager in Saigon.

"You will never be rich if you buy a car," I say.

"Interesting," he says.

Julie compliments him on his command of English and apologizes for our not knowing Vietnamese.

"You learn Vietnamese?" he asks. "Why?" Then he says, "English is my future."

10

There is little awareness in Vietnam that the country has few oilfields to exploit, or that oil might someday become too expensive for its economy, or that even if Vietnam were to have access to unlimited cheap oil, its economy won't grow by 7 percent year after year forever. There is no realization that recent floods in the central part of the country might be related to changes in the world climate, or that the rice fields of the Mekong Delta could be under the South China Sea in a few decades. There is no fear that tourists might stop coming from Europe and America. Population growth is seen as a problem by a few government officials, but when Vietnam's official two-child policy was recently relaxed, it took only a year for the population growth rate to almost double.

Where it's not being used as material for concrete buildings, the whole country is being cleared and terraced to grow vegetables, using farming methods practiced for millennia. Vietnam will still have agriculture if industrialism and globalism and world currencies implode. But it's not hard to imagine the great tourist hotels becoming high-rise versions of the jungle-covered temples of Angkor Wat.

As for the young people who have put their faith in our cherished Western narrative of hard work and accumulated wealth, I think there will come a time when they will be angry and disappointed for themselves and their families. At least they won't starve, I think, but then I remember that when the Japanese confiscated the Vietnamese rice crop in 1945, two million of them did.

Near the end of our time in Vietnam, Julie and I hike to a high peak outside the city of Dalat. It's a long way, and a warm day, and on our way back down we stop at a roadside café. A wizened old woman sells us two cans of Coke and sits down at our table. She looks at our wedding rings and smiles.

"How many?" she asks. She searches for an English word. "Kids," she says, finally.

Julie shakes her head no. She draws a zero on the tabletop with the moisture from her Coke can.

I say that we're content to be uncle and aunt, but that doesn't get across at all.

"I have eleven kids," she says. "My kids have ten kids."

She asks me my age and I tell her, but I add that this is my first trip to Vietnam. I think she understands what I mean by that.

"I am . . ." she says, pauses, shrugs, and draws a 62 on the tabletop.

I want to start joking with her, telling her she's younger than me but is two generations older than me. I want to tell her we could have gone to high school together. I want to tell her that twenty-one descendants is maybe too many for one person. None of that is going to translate.

We smile at each other in silence for a while, and then I pay her for the Cokes and get up to leave.

"No children," she says. "No grandchildren." She shakes her head in pity and mimes a clown's exaggerated sadness.

I want to tell her to save her tears for her own children and grandchildren. I want to tell her that a hundred million children and grandchildren is too many for her country, and that the airplanes loaded with Coke-drinking tourists will not always show up. I want to tell her that she's on the wrong end of history's largest taxi scam, and that the South Korean and Chinese and American investors in Vietnam are going to want loan sharks' returns on their investments. I want to tell her that her grandchildren are already seen as someone else's wealth, and that her mountains are being eaten.

These things would be hard to translate, even if I spoke her language or if she knew more than a few words of mine.

What would be impossible to translate—what would look like crazy—is my dawning realization that Vietnam didn't win the Vietnam War.

It took us thirty years. But when the first American tourist got off a jet in Hanoi, wearing a Hawaiian shirt and carrying a Nikon, he was the point of a new spear, carrying more money than any ten Russians, and pictures of an American house and an American car, and maybe a photo of himself or a brother or a friend in uniform, and an inked spot on a map where an obscure battle was fought. He thought that people might be interested in these things, and they were. Maybe he apologized for his government's carpet bombing and spraying of Agent Orange. Maybe he called Saigon Ho Chi Minh City until he realized he was the only one south of Hanoi calling it that.

Maybe he hired an old NVA soldier for a guide, and maybe he struck up a friendship with his former enemy. Maybe he offered to invest in a country that needed to rebuild a ruined infrastructure and put millions of unemployed young people to work. Maybe he appealed to their hopes for their children and grandchildren. Maybe his unconscious sense of privilege was noticed by a people acutely conscious of privilege. Maybe he said—just as unconsciously—that with the right loans and business practices, they and their families could be rich, too.

The conquest was complete in a decade.

is civilization too dumb to live?

*That you've made it this
far means you're smart, right?*

1

In his 1951 short story, "The Marching Morons," the science-fiction writer C. M. Kornbluth postulates a far future where, for generations, people of high intelligence have rarely had children and people of low intelligence have had as many as they can. As a result, the world average IQ is 45. Five billion stupid folks sit around, watch TV, and go to jobs where if they screw up it won't hurt anything, while a few hundred thousand smart ones work desperately to keep civilization going.

Then a salesman of twentieth-century Florida swampland awakes from several millennia of suspended animation, the result of an electrochemical accident in a dentist's office. Once he figures out what's going on, he offers the intelligent people a solution to their problem: all the stupid people can be tricked into boarding rocket ships bound for Venus. He designs brochures that show it as a tropical paradise where canned ham grows on trees.

The rockets are built and boarded. The ships, having been built by morons, miss Venus and disappear into the sun.

When all the stupid people are gone, the smart ones, free of their charges but hating the salesman for the solution he gave them, put him in the final rocket. The world is empty, except for a bunch of remorseful killers with IQs of 175 or so.

I first read this story when I was sixteen. As a student who did well on standardized tests, I liked it. At the time I believed in a cheery social Darwinism where students who tested well rose to the top of the American meritocracy, became rich and famous, and drove Mustang GTs. The story even gave those students a conscience, but only after they had gotten rid of all the stupid people cluttering their lives.

I recently read the story again. I don't like it nearly as well as I did when I was an Ayn Rand fan.

For one thing, the IQ tests that I aced as a high schooler have been designed to produce a perfect bell curve of results. The average IQ is 100 by definition, and it occupies the top of the curve. Half of any group of test subjects will be below average in intelligence. Half will be above.

But there's a problem with that perfect curve, and it's a big one. Forcing anybody's intelligence to fit a theoretical construct is an act of statistical violence. IQ tests compress lots of discrete intelligences down to a cryptic two- or three-digit number that pays no attention to empathy, intuition, or emotional awareness. Intelligence testing reduces human beings to numbers, and the lowest of these numbers become expendable in the eyes of amateur social engineers like Kornbluth's salesman of soggy Florida real estate.

Also note that the term *moron* didn't spring into existence with the blogosphere. It was coined in 1910 by the American Association for the Study of the Feeble-Minded (not called that anymore, even in the blogosphere) to indicate persons with a mental age of seven to twelve. It was considered a medical term until it was adopted by the general public as an insult. Even worse, it was appropriated by early twentieth-century American eugenicists, those optimistic pseudoscientists who aimed to control human breeding to promote desirable traits. What happened next can be seen, from our temporal perspective, as what you get when you combine a really bad idea with really bad people.

Kornbluth's story isn't really science fiction. Six years prior to its publication, the Nazis were marching people they considered defective into gas chambers disguised as showers, a low-tech version of people-packed Venus rockets. To recapitulate the Holocaust with a satirical science-fiction story was, at the least, adolescent bad taste. But adolescent bad taste didn't bother me when I was an adolescent.

These days, I'm bothered. I'm also bothered that genocide isn't an aberration in human history, although it was an aberration that the Jews were better educated than the Nazis. It bothers me that Kornbluth, reaching for a world-population figure beyond all human tolerance, came up with a little over five billion, two-and-a-half billion fewer than we've got now.

It bothers me that the United States of America is not a meritocracy, even the kind of one I thought it was when I was in high school. Instead, the USA has been, sometimes all at once, an oligarchy, a gerontocracy, a kleptocracy, a corporatocracy, and a moronocracy.

It bothers me to use the word *moron*, although not so much that I don't reach for it when someone displays toxic deficiencies in judgment, honesty, or empathy. Kornbluth used it to evoke the crime of making some humans expendable so other humans could have their stuff. It expressed his considerable anger at a civilization that was destroying itself as he watched.

Here's the difficult fact: as much as we all might like to live in a world where smart people run things, we don't. Our legislative chambers and executive offices aren't teeming with geniuses, and even the Deep State, should you choose to believe in it, seems at best a cabal of the cognitively challenged.

Maybe our political and business leaders started out smart and became stupid because they were running things, because power makes you stupid. Stealing makes you stupid, and there's plenty of theft, petty and otherwise, going on in the halls of power. Stealing also requires lying to yourself and others, and lying makes you really stupid.

And certainly age makes you stupid, which is something that also concerns me more than it did fifty years ago. The typical American seventy-two-year-old male has the same size brain he had when he was three. Women's brains don't seem to shrink as much with age, but that's probably because they're not running things or stealing or lying as much as men. When you look at all the old people in positions of power, it's hard not to see them as a collection of shrunken brains doing what they do best, which is shrinking.

The most disturbing realization that Kornbluth's story brings up for me now is that being smart doesn't mean you have any innate ability to improve the lives of other people. In fact, if you look at the smart people who designed America's banking system, or wrote torture memos, or ran their companies into the ground, or offshored jobs, or tore children away from their parents, or supplied weapons to Saudi Arabia, or prescribed terribly addictive opioids to people with minor back pain, it doesn't seem as if these folks' undoubtedly high scores on IQ tests indicate any capacity for grief, pity, or appreciation of the down-the-line effects of their actions on others.

It's an indelicate question for me to ask, but you might ask yourself if you have a rocket-to-Venus equivalent in your life, and whether you've strapped yourself into one of its seats, and where it is that you're really headed.

A canned-ham paradise, I know. An exclusive retirement community.

As I write, I worry that a sixteen-year-old summer intern in a Big Pharma biolab with a straight-A average in his STEM classes and a habit of rereading *Atlas Shrugged* is injecting bird flu into a lab animal with Zika virus, just to see what will happen. As for Kornbluth's "The Marching Morons," he's read it, too, and he thinks it's about him, but in a good way.

2

My library contains books on plagues, biowarfare, and tropical diseases. Most of them came from the Barnes & Noble remainder bin, which indicates that their publishers expected to sell more of these books than they did. Apparently, people don't like reading books about bedbug-vectored Chagas' disease or smallpox-loaded artillery shells or more frequent Ebola breakouts as the wild world is converted to cities and farms.

But I buy these books. I appreciate the 80 percent discount. I don't find their subject matter cheering, but I like to keep up with what's happening in medical science and its weaponized offspring.

I've been interested in such matters since 1980. That year, as part of an interview for a job as a medical writer, I was asked to translate an article on recombinant DNA and monoclonal antibodies, written in near-opaque medicalese, into blunt-force everyday English.

The article described the mechanism by which microorganisms could be made to produce interferon, which was supposed to be a cure for cancer. It wasn't, but nobody knew that then. Instead, medicine was seen as being on the verge of singular breakthroughs. Physical immortality was just a few designer proteins away.

My translation got me the job, and I ended up writing a book about myocardial infarcts called *So You've Gone and Had a Heart Attack*. I learned that when you put medicalese into understandable language, a lot of medicine consists of common sense, prevention, and coming to terms with the knowledge that the human body—whatever designer proteins you inject into it—grows old and falls apart.

I also learned that almost every medical study is subject to the Law of Unintended Consequences, which is what happens when your results refuse to exist in the same universe with your study parameters.

The most important thing I learned was that the language used to propose, run, and interpret a study was a determining factor in how well the study held up over time. The better writers did better science, which is to say that good writing is the most important parameter of any study, even when it's not seen as a parameter.

The company I worked for was abandoned by its venture capitalists before my book was ever published. People in focus groups said they did not want to buy books that explained their diseases in blunt-force everyday English. They preferred to place their health in the hands of experts who spoke in a language they did not understand and who prescribed drugs whose efficacy declined with familiarity.

Still, medical science marches on. And what do you do when you can operate on a bacterium and change its mechanisms to produce a new protein? Do you sit back and say, "Well, interferon didn't work out the way we'd hoped, so we'll just quit and go back to treating cancer with surgery and radiation"?

Of course not. You start looking for other proteins, enzymes, and bioactive lipids. Once you've turned your E. coli buddies into little interferon factories, your next move is to retool their assembly lines to make other complex molecules, some of them plucked from the immune systems of the patients you're treating, and hope that one of them will be more effective against cancer. Or heart disease. Or death.

Lots of venture capitalists are waiting for the molecule that will be effective against death.

3

The exponential growth in human population that marked the twentieth century was made possible by antibiotics, advances in sanitation, more abundant food supplies, fossil-fueled transport, an exponential expansion of resource extraction, and go-forth-and-multiply religions and governments. The current human population is an improbable and dangerous mix of technology, energy, and ideology.

Take away oil, coal, fertilizer, medicines, credit, chainsaws, bulldozers, cement plants, pipelines, container ships, and the pervasive screens that allow the preferred contemporary human environment to be made up largely of pixels, and you face the reduction of human numbers to preindustrial levels in less than a decade.

If studies of animal population explosions followed by population crashes—the passenger pigeon, the reindeer on St. Matthew Island, and the deer on the Kaibab Plateau are textbook examples—can be extrapolated to humans, our population decline will reduce our numbers to five hundred million or fewer. Way fewer, if the mechanism of decline involves war between starving people.

In practical terms, technological civilization is holding seven billion of us hostage. Either it continues, or those of us who depend on civilized jobs, civilized energy, civilized social structures, and civilized roofs over our heads will die. If the wars in

Yemen and South Sudan are any indication, children will go first.

People who say that our world isn't a fatally flawed human artifact, who say civilization will always find plenty of energy, who say capitalism will continue to expand in a world of finite resources, are suffering from the techno-industrial equivalent of Stockholm syndrome. Either that, or they're all morons.

4

Consider a coal mine in Wales.

When the mine was discovered, coal seams lay on the surface, and it was a simple matter to dig pits and short tunnels to get enough coal to burn in hearths and crude smelters. Over time, those tunnels and pits deepened, and the energy needed to get coal to the surface increased. Humans carrying baskets of coal up ladders were replaced by draft animals turning windlasses or pulling slip scrapers. Tunnels and pits deepened further. Demand for coal increased as smelters grew larger and began to use coking technology.

Enter the steam engine, a giant machine with a huge riveted cast-iron boiler and a vast coal-burning firebox. Its barrel-sized pistons wheezed and hissed and drove cast-iron wheels that powered pumps and drilling equipment in coal deposits hundreds of yards below the surface of the earth. Other steam engines in factories, railroad locomotives, and ships demanded more and more coal. Profits spurred improvements in mining technology.

When steam engines were connected to generators, the belts and shafts and compressed air hoses that had transferred power from the steam engine to the coal face were no longer needed. Giant electrical shovels and drills and coal trucks in deep pits were safer and more efficient than miners in tunnels.

Pistons were replaced by steam turbines, but the fuel that powered the mining machinery was still what the mine mined.

Exponential production curves worked their wonders, and the coal ran out sooner than expected. Mine maintenance slowed, then stopped. When its pumps were turned off, the mine filled with dark water. The company town emptied. A few years later all that was left was a smoke-blackened landscape marked by poisonous streams, piles of ash and waste rock, and the picked-over remains of machines too big or too obsolete to move.

Still, after a generation, vegetation began to reappear on bare and eroded hillsides. The blackened foundations of miners' houses began to shelter small trees, and the wild descendants of once-tended roses began to form thorny thickets. Animals denned in old boilers and moss grew in the dark interiors of old fireboxes. The place began to have a kind of delicate archaeological beauty. It wasn't at the level of temples overgrown with jungle, but it was enough to allow sensitive visitors to contemplate the conversations, hopes, lives, and deaths of miners and their families and the lives and deaths of those who had managed them, and to reflect on the decline and fall of institutions based on one prudent decision at a time.

5

Consider the earth as a coal mine in Wales.

6

I live in a part of America—like a lot of parts of America— where men and women keep arsenals in their basements. There is a psychology of previous investment here, where people who have spent most of a decade's discretionary income on guns and ammunition and freeze-dried food keep buying more and more guns and ammunition and freeze-dried food and giving time and effort to imagining the scenarios that make them necessary. Civilization's collapse is looked forward to, not because it will end our destruction of the world and our fellow creatures, but because it validates an I'm-going-to-live-you're-going-to-die mind-set. That's the headspace a lot of people happily occupy after a decade of preparing for collapse.

Four-year-olds in towns near my home have wardrobes that include body armor—these are kids that as they grow, they molt. Their parents have basements and crawl spaces full of food, and visions of our local mountains as defensible walls. They plan to fell trees across roads and blow up bridges and shoot the bad people who still try to push their way into the valley. Those bad people will look like ordinary suburban Americans a week or two after the supermarkets are empty and the gas stations are dry and the electricity has been turned off.

I don't spend a lot of time in our local saloons, but when I do I overhear barstool arguments about Building 7 collapsing all by itself on 9/11, or about the handful of bloodstained bullets found on the floor of JFK's limousine, or about the merits of a scoped 30-06 BAR loaded with World War II surplus armor-piercing ammunition versus an open-sight .308 assault rifle with a twenty-round clip. Which one will be better against a mob of starving urban refugees and their children?

My usual contribution to these discussions is to ask, from down the bar, "What about germs?"

"Huh?"

"What about biowarfare? Don't you think the Deep State will release weaponized smallpox into the population? Don't you think there are plans to deal with people who are preparing for civil war? You think they'd go to all the trouble to put militia members in concentration camps and feed them surplus cheese? There isn't going to be surplus cheese. The Deep State likes cheese. It's going to come after the freeze-dried cheese you're hiding in your basement. It'll help if you're already dead of smallpox or something else it's got in the freezer. All that money you spent on ammunition? Should have bought a hazmat suit. I'm sure they make them for children."

Hooded eyes turn to me from a distance measured in empty beer glasses. "Keep talking, Deep Stater. Enjoy the time you've got left. When civil authority evaporates, you'll be the first to go."

7

It's not good for your long-term well-being to mess with the minds of paranoid survivalists. But if you want to know what's really going down, it's useful to bring Occam's razor to bear on theories that require hundreds of faithful secret keepers or the perfect step-by-step execution of the malignant intentions of alien lizards who walk among us in human suits. If you think the Masons, the Bilderbergers, the Bohemian Club, or the Deep State are running things behind the scenes, it's instructive to look at the complex multigenerational logistics involved, particularly when one of those generations— mine—is otherwise wrecking the world its children will have to live in.

Occam's razor is a way of choosing one hypothesis over another. It states that in the absence of certainty, you should prefer the explanation with the fewest number of variables. In practice, this means the simplest explanation is usually the right one.

An example much used to illustrate Occam's razor is the replacement of the Ptolemaic view of the cosmos by the

Copernican view. It is simpler to place the sun at the center of the solar system rather than the earth, even though astronomers could construct complex mechanical models of the Ptolemaic solar system that explained the night sky just as well as Copernicus's theory.

As long as one's perspective was confined to earth, that is. Once we were able to set cameras and transmitters in orbit around the earth and sun, we had photographic evidence that Copernicus was right.

Unless, of course, the moon landing was done in a Hollywood studio. Unless those rockets blasting off from the Baikonur Cosmodrome are all scheduled to miss the International Space Station and plunge into the sun. Unless the complex formulas used to slingshot Voyager I and II around the planets and out of the solar system were mathematical nonsense cooked up in a Madison Avenue advertising agency by hard-charging guys who drank martinis and drove Porsches and had affairs with their secretaries, never thinking to lift their eyes above their concrete-and-steel horizon.

I have faith in Occam's razor, myself. Here's my simple hypothesis on these matters: we live on a planet that gravity has shaped into a sphere, and that sphere isn't infinite. Our global civilization is running into limits on essential resources and other limits on where to put our garbage. These limits, when apprehended by brains formed by a quarter-million years of tribal living, spark tribal solutions: financial and political favoritism, scapegoating, appeals to the dark gods of vengeance, and a breakdown of civility between people who heretofore have tolerated each other.

In other words, people who seemed highly intelligent when our civilization was growing and thriving turn into morons when economies slow and threaten to go in reverse.

People who should know better put corporate profits above

the health of children, support government shutdowns, and get in fistfights with former astronauts. Their kids have to sneak out of the house to get vaccinated. Whole swaths of the population, experiencing personal and familial and cognitive disaster long before the rest of us are aware it's happening, vote for people who promise to raze once-venerated institutions to the ground rather than try to repair what's broken.

A civilization going ka-ka in its own nest? An unwitting—by definition—conspiracy of morons? Believe me, it's the simplest explanation.

8

When I think about the time between now and 2030, I look at all the countries sitting on stocks of anthrax and smallpox and nuclear and chemical weapons, signed treaties notwithstanding. I think of India and Pakistan: two nations who well and truly hate each other are getting to the point where one brighter-than-a-thousand-suns day of 150 million deaths is preferable to sharing the world with each other. I think of the Aum Shinrikyo religion, stymied in its effort to cause mass death in the Tokyo subway system by sarin gas distribution problems, problems that were completely solved by the world's militaries fifty years ago. I think of Kim Jong Un, sitting on North Korea's fifty or so nuclear bombs, and the average length of Donald Trump's friendships.

These worries are symptoms of a deeper worry, which is my fear that no nation will survive the general inability to think occasioned by the failure of its finances, a lethal climate, and a steep decline in energy supplies.

I worry that the present will turn out to be far kinder than the future. Even in these last days of what might be called a global conscience, the most oppressive states manage to give meaning and comfort to a majority of their citizens. They treat their women and children and the old as people, not useless eaters. They don't turn every one of their young men into killers. They pay lip service to ethics and altruism, and sometimes the rule of law.

If that lip service comes to an end, as it will if authoritarians end up leading the surviving nation-states of the world, it will add to the numbers of the morons who voted them into office or allowed them to be voted into office. At some point in the trajectory of authoritarianism, even smart people begin acting like morons in an act of protective morphology.

9

One of the appalling characteristics of people who take their own virtue for granted is a refusal to think about the evil they might commit simply by trying to help out friends, family, and neighbors. Or if they think about it, they don't see it as evil.

The effect of this blindness is to give bad people an excuse to see themselves as good as long as being bad benefits their tribe.

Biological warfare isn't just idle bar talk. Since the 1950s it's been a ready-to-implement solution to the problem of declining resources. Find a disease you can vaccinate against, inoculate the people you still want to hang out with, and release it in the world's airports. A few months later you and those aforementioned friends, family, and neighbors have oil and food and property in abundance. But your humanity would have to be destroyed before you could commit that unspeakable evil, right?

I'd like to think so. I'd like to be able to forget the damage done to humanity by the folks who gave smallpox-infected blankets to American Indians in 1763, and the Japanese who dropped plague bacillus on Chinese cities in World War II. I'd like to have never found out about the Russian and American programs that produced tons of anthrax spores before a 1972 treaty made them quit it. I'd like to be able to pretend that people never weaponized pneumonic tularemia or hardened smallpox against antibiotics.

But biological warfare is a possibility, no matter how it twists our idea of what a human being is capable of. In fact, judging by the deliberate exposure of scientific illiterates to anti-vaccination memes, and the de facto denial of preventive medical services to the poor, it's happening here and now.

Conventional morality suggests that only people so incomprehensibly evil as to be inhuman—Kornbluth's revived real-estate salesman seems to fit the description—could deliberately release pathogens into the human environment, or start a nuclear war, or smuggle nerve agents across international borders in perfume bottles. But the evidence indicates that evil isn't the province of the inhuman. Any of us, given the right circumstances, could be as evil as all that, especially if it doesn't require any effort.

It's just as effective to ignore people who are starving and dying of disease than to dehumanize and then murder them. Deny jobs, housing, medical resources and food to the poor folks who bother you, and eventually they will go away. With enough patience and enough freeze-dried chicken stroganoff in your basement, you'll still get all their stuff.

10

To further our discussion of evil, we might combine Occam's razor with Fermi's paradox. Fermi's paradox suggests that the galaxy should be full of civilizations, since 100 billion stars, almost all of them orbited by planets, should give rise to intelligent life at least some of the time. A percentage of those intelligences should give rise to technological civilizations. If one in a million stars produces such a civilization, that's a hundred thousand civilizations that should have ham radio operators. Yet we haven't heard any evidence of anybody else out there.

Elaborate explanations have been proposed for our cosmic solitude, including the idea that we're an incurably malignant species and have been put in permanent quarantine. But there's a simpler answer: intelligence progresses on a planet until it invents an industrial revolution, complete with a resource extraction–based capitalist economy—in essence, a heat engine with billions of moving parts. After a few hundred revolutions of the planet around its star, the engine blows up and wrecks its biosphere and everything in it.

In the end it doesn't make much difference who's intelligent and who isn't. The vast silence that has greeted our SETI antennae has a simple message: *You're Next.*

Whether we end up with a Venus-style molten-lead climate or revert back to being nasty and brutish and short hunter-scavengers living parasite-ridden lives amid the wet and moldy ruins of once-great cities, the result will be the death of thought. These two paths are not that different, really, if you imagine yourself listening to nothing but the hiss of static and pondering Fermi's paradox from a thousand light-years away, as a member of a civilization that made it a few more years into the future than we did.

eating with peter singer

How much happiness can one planet stand?

1

A subversive act I committed as a college professor was to introduce my first-year composition students to Jeremy Bentham, the University College of London philosopher who gave the world Utilitarianism. I did it because my students were supposed to be learning to think critically.

Critical thinking and Utilitarianism are not always antagonists, but they often are. Governments have killed lots of people in the name of the greatest happiness for the greatest number, and that's the sort of thing that fires up critical thinkers everywhere. But that's not where I began my introduction.

Instead, I talked about Bentham's 1832 will and testament, which specified that his body was to be dissected and then transformed into an auto-icon, a lifelike representation of the person he had been while living. His head was to be mummified using the expertise of the recently contacted New Zealand Maoris. His skeleton, once flensed, was to be padded with hay and dressed in a formal suit, including underwear and shoes stuffed with two pairs of socks. The figure was to be seated on a favorite chair in a glass-fronted case. The preserved head, complete with lifelike glass eyes, was to be reattached to its backbone. Anyone looking into the case was supposed to see what a nineteenth-century philosopher of happiness looked like.

Everything but the mummification of the head went as planned. Photos of the head available on the Internet show what happens when taxidermists aspire to zombie porn. Its blue glass eyes seek you out no matter how far you are from your screen. Its bleached-orange skin has shrunk to fit the skull beneath it. Its nose is a corroded and blackened bit of cartilage. Its wispy hair hovers over its brow like swamp gas. The ears, at least, look like any other old man's ears, which doesn't help as much as you might think.

Good taste—at least relatively good taste—prevailed. A wax head, with a face that more resembled the living Bentham, was attached to the skeleton, completing the auto-icon. The real head was put in a box tucked under the chair. The case and auto-icon, the latter a little worse for the passage of time and the presence of carpet-beetles, are still displayed at University College. The mummified head has been placed in a secure room in the Archaeology Department, and you have to have an exceptional reason—and exceptional predilections, I suspect—to see it.

At this point, the story slips toward the apocryphal. Legend has it that the auto-icon was wheeled into faculty council meetings, where it was registered as "Jeremy Bentham, present but non-voting," except in cases of a tie, where it always voted aye, whatever the question. Rival King's College students are supposed to have kidnapped the mummified head and played football with it. The head was stolen and found in a railway storage locker in Scotland. The head was stolen and ransomed, with ten pounds going to a charity for its return. The head was Bentham's enthusiastic nod to medical experimentation on cadavers. The head was a posthumous joke on posterity, even though Bentham was not known for his sense of humor.

Students liked hearing about Bentham, but before the class was over, I would always quote his 1776 definition of Utilitarianism, which was that "the greatest happiness for the greatest number is the measure of right and wrong." That sentence is a mind worm. It enters your ear and chews its way to your brain, where over years it separates the gray matter into its components of black and white. It creates a kind of true believer, because it reduces all human problems to an equation, and then it solves the equation for any value of x.

You can't argue with happiness, at least if it's your own, but I cautioned my students against becoming uncritical Utilitarians. I asked them to instead write three or four pages explaining why Jeremy Bentham's philosophy was just as horrifying as his beetle-bitten head. If they didn't think Utilitarianism was horrifying, they had to do enough research to convince me otherwise.

2

If the greatest happiness for the greatest number is the greatest good, goodness has prevailed beyond Bentham's wildest dreams. More people are living better now than at any other time in human history. China has finally lifted more people out of poverty than it murdered during the Cultural Revolution. Vaccination programs are saving billions of children from dozens of life-wrecking diseases. Women have access to education and legal protections denied to them since hunter-gatherer days. Criminals are safely in jail, for our happiness and their longevity—millions of them.

To a large degree, the world pays lip service to Bentham's stands against slavery and for humane prisons, his advocacy of equal treatment for all humans, his arguments for the merciful processing of animals, his vision of a body politic governed by benign self-interest, and his conviction that reason-guided technology could progressively solve humanity's dolor. His definition of pleasure as the absence of pain has been elevated to medical truth.

These were the Utilitarian virtues I asked my students to go up against, and, understandably, most of them didn't want to. They wrote that Bentham's philosophy was a good thing in spite of what he had arranged for his head. They wished they had thought of it themselves—the philosophy, that is.

A few of them were uncomfortable with the idea of the tyranny of the majority, which I had mentioned as one of Utilitarianism's vices. A few of them began to worry when they realized that Bentham's egalitarianism had implications for which and how many people they should love and nourish. Some of them, looking into the idea of reason as the sole guide for action, noted that reason can be a cramped and unforgiving place.

Some fewer were perceptive enough to question who the greatest number referred to, and who determined who was a who and who wasn't a who. One or two found that a sorority or fraternity had become a tyrannical majority in their lives.

A nontraditional student, back for an undergraduate degree after working as a nurse's aide, followed her research to Bentham's humane prison, his panopticon. She found Foucault's critique of Bentham's bright-lit idea, and she drew disturbing parallels between a prison that afforded no privacy and the industrial treatment of patients in the hospital she had worked in. Another nontraditional student, an ex-cop working in campus security, connected, with considerable prescience, Bentham's absence of pain with the heroin addicts that were beginning to show up on the streets of our pastoral college town.

In spite of these insights, my assignment was a failure. It

didn't work unless you had some real-world experience, which was in short supply among the eighteen-year-olds who made up the greatest number of the class.

If I were to assign the essay again, I'd ask the students to write a letter to the University College Archaeology Department giving the reasons they should be allowed to open the safe containing Jeremy Bentham's mummified head and cradle it in their laps. Think critically about *this*, I would say.

It's the face of human extinction, I would say.

By way of explanation, I would tell them that if you want to blame any one person for humanity's inability to deal with the lethal feedback loops it has set in motion, you could do worse than to look at Jeremy Bentham. A world tyrannized by the majority—especially if that majority consists of poor people watching the limousine of prosperity head for the ditch just as they've jumped on its running boards—will keep industrial capitalism going as long as possible, no matter the collateral damage.

Smartphones and personal electronic assistants and their utilization by the current authoritarian governments have made what Foucault said about the panopticon—that Bentham had given us a vision of invisible, total, soul-deficient social control—look a bit Pollyanna-ish.

Also, the greatest happiness for the greatest number has run smack into what might be called, in Western terms, the dilemma of Jainism. Jainism, an ascetic sect of Hinduism, prohibits harming any living being, which inflates Bentham's greatest number considerably. It makes the strictest asceticism not strict enough. It makes an animal-based diet a matter of crippling guilt. It makes a two-by-four into the synecdoche of a destroyed forest. It makes a single bottle of amoxycillin a prescription for mass murder.

On the other end of the greatest-number spectrum are

tribes of one, people for whom the greatest number is the number one-ber, regardless of the fact that it's also the loneliest. These people will sacrifice anybody, or a bunch of anybodies, for the greater good, which is, in their minds, them.

In the middle are not-well-thought-out ideas about who gets to be in the tribe that counts. Blue-eyed Aryans made the cut in Hitler's Germany. In our local bars, it's people who have prepared for collapse (the ants as opposed to the grasshoppers). In economics departments, it's the middle class, the upper class, or the lower class, depending on the politics of the PhD committee. In Mid-East studies, it's the Israelis or Palestinians, but seldom both at once. In baseball it's Yankee fans, no matter how many World Series the Red Sox win. In originalist America, it's male landowners. In the American South, it's people who possess proper ID. Many of the people on this list think that it would be just fine if they were the only people on the list.

3

I hoped to convince my undergraduate charges to be careful about ideologies masquerading as moral imperatives. Toward the end of the semester, having softened them up with Bentham, I introduced them to the thinking of Peter Singer, a contemporary proponent of the greatest lack of suffering for the greatest number.

Singer is a bioethicist and philosopher at Princeton University who argues that animals are sentient, empathetic, and, in effect, people. Lots of cat and dog owners will agree with him. But once you embrace dogs and cats as people, Singer expands the category.

Singer suggests that because animals—not dogs and cats, but still-personable cows and sheep, pigs, horses, geese, and chickens—act unhappy and terrified as they're slaughtered for food, it causes more suffering for farmed animals to give their lives to become meat than it does for humans to quit gorging themselves on rib steak, rack of lamb, chicken salad, pork loin, and foie gras.

In "The Singer Solution to World Poverty," a *New York Times* article I assigned to my students, Singer notes that most NYT readers live a life of plenty in a world where other humans starve. Singer suggests evil finds a foothold in our hearts when, say, forty dollars buys us a bottle of wine at Costco instead of feeding three or four malnourished southern-hemisphere children for a month.

Singer knows whereof he speaks. By deeply conservative estimates, ten million people die of starvation every year in this world, and that's not including recent war-generated famines like the ones in Yemen and South Sudan.

They're not starving just because their communities lack a Costco. It's not from a failure of the markets, either, because those markets have diverted an enormous amount of corn into the production of ethanol, which means the price of food has gone beyond the reach of some people so other people will have cheaper gasoline, which they can burn on automobile trips to Costco, where they buy whole cases of forty-dollar wine, the equivalent of many more of Singer's starving southern-hemisphere children.

Singer delights in taking instances of singular evil—say, an SS officer, whip in hand, driving terrified and unhappy people into an underground chamber, which is then pumped full of Zyklon B gas—and pointing out that such evil isn't singular at all. It's possible to equate that Nazi officer with a wealthy American choosing to have three or four children, as it's likely that those children will grow up and buy wine, thereby brutally ending the lives of their below-the-equator counterparts.

Indirect guilt becomes direct responsibility in Singer's writings, and he uses a simple algebra in his calculations of evil. If the unit of evil is x, representing the murder, by whatever means, of one person, the worldwide free market is responsible for ten million x per year. That's because it produces superyachts and Aston Martins and Cartier handbags rather than nutritious meals for starving people. If I'm reading Singer correctly, that makes global markets twice as evil per year as Hitler, who only averaged five million murders for every year he was in power.

Singer denies his readers easy moral solutions. You can't simply send forty dollars to a children's aid organization and then buy your wine, because now the wine has become an eighty-dollar bottle of wine, whose price would feed *six or eight* starving children for a month.

My students didn't like reading Singer. He redefined their consumption as criminal, their impulses toward cars and clothes and bacon as murder. He gave the lie to any pretensions they had of going through life in an ethical way.

Singer's own ethics are statistically impeccable, but he sparked a round of ad hominem attacks from my students. He was criticized for expecting the impossible and being unforgiving when anyone failed to achieve it. My poorer students noted that he was a part of a university system that had impoverished them with college loans. Once again, my nontraditional students came through with an appropriate contrarian argument, wondering if Singer, by advocating sacrifices that they found impossible to make and would happily forget as soon as class ended, wasn't functioning as a de facto apologist for the inequality he decried.

Here's my own evasion of Singer's imperatives, courtesy of the Second Law: Singer's moral consciousness is an inevitability, the kind of self-organizing system that feeds on energy freed up when concentrated energy sources, such as the Princeton University endowment, begin to dissipate. Singer dissipates energy in turn by running around urging well-meaning Americans to give twenty thousand of every fifty thousand dollars they make to people in deep poverty. If those Americans dissipate their energy in the direction of the poor, then those no-longer-poor people, with money for the first time in their lives, use it to acquire food and energy. When they reach their new, higher limits of organization and resources, they dissipate them in turn. In the end, all these self-organizing systems themselves dissipate. The imperative here is not moral. It's entropic.

I'm not the first person who has intellectualized an escape from a moral dilemma.

But you still wonder if anyone will promote any ethics if money and fossil fuels go away. In blunt terms, worrying about whether or not animals are people is a level of ethical thought possible only when you have a full stomach and a tight roof. Get cold and hungry, and even people start looking like—well, animals. Tasty, cookable, dissipate-able animals.

4

I've just come back from a trip to the Boise Costco, and from the healthy sizes of the humans in its aisles, it will be a long time before starvation will trump ethics in my neck of the woods. But something is trumping ethics, there in those crowded aisles of leather furniture, foreign cheeses, plastic-wrapped animal parts, Vietnamese sweatshop clothing, cell phones, giant flat TVs, motor oil and tires, patio furniture, five-bladed razor cartridges, vitamin supplements, bulk coffee, southern-hemisphere fruits and vegetables, robot-created oil paintings of blue-eyed, blond Jesuses—the carts carrying this stuff leave every Costco big box in a steady stream.

Stand by the outlet of your nearest Costco, right next to the giant Chevy four-wheel-drive four-door pickup on sale only to Costco members, and you'll watch the lives of a lot of southern-hemisphere children blotted out each time a fluorescent marker slashes down through a cash-register receipt. Then go across the parking lot to gas up your car for the ride home, because nobody has better prices for fossil fuel.

After reading Peter Singer with my students, I've concluded that doing the right thing and using my Costco card require that I not think about them at the same time. If I do, going to Costco becomes an exercise in pain and guilt, things I usually go to Costco to avoid.

I of course know that starving children and bits of once-sentient critters in huge refrigerated bins in the Costco meat department exist in the same world, and that conjunction in itself makes for a painful moral paradox.

Singer doesn't dwell in gray areas. He indicates that every time I drive the 140 miles to the nearest Costco and come home with the trunk lid squeezing down all that I've bought, I'm killing creatures whose only sin is to want to live.

It's not that I disbelieve Peter Singer. I believe him. So do lots of other people who behave as I do.

Singer's arguments haven't convinced most middle-class Americans that they need to alleviate the suffering of animals. He hasn't convinced lawmakers to require starving children equivalents on wine labels. He hasn't even convinced me to stop buying wine.

In fact, halfway through a bottle of pinot noir, I stop worrying about Peter Singer's imperatives and start getting moody about Jeremy Bentham's head. I start giving imaginary writing assignments to long-graduated students, who must by now be in the middle of raising children and consulting retirement advisors. I doubt that my exposing them to Singer's ethics has produced notable growth in their charity budgets. I doubt that they're spending much time writing.

That doesn't stop me from deciding to tell them, from the memory-lectern of a long-ago classroom, to write down what they'd say to Jeremy Bentham's head once they've got hold of it. And then, since there's no one around to complete the assignment but me, I do it myself.

"Things have changed a bit since mummification, Jeremy. The amount of easily extracted whale oil has been determined to be limited, and burning coal to power steam engines produces carbon dioxide, which you know as 'dead air'—which isn't a bad name for it in its projected concentrations. The atmosphere and the oceans can only absorb so much carbon dioxide before the climate gets lethal.

"But we don't asphyxiate, not at first. We overheat, or die in weather accidents, or drown in rainstorms due to an out-of-control warming phenomenon discovered decades after you died. As much as you might yearn for a little warmth in your English winters, when it actually happens it comes with nasty side effects.

"Also, too little oil and too much carbon dioxide means two hundred years of growing and thriving, of ever greater happiness and ever greater numbers—everything you said could happen, and did—could slow, stop, or go into reverse. Civilizations have recessions and depressions when they slow down, and when they start shrinking, we start looking, through our own glassy eyes, at the greatest pain for the greatest number.

"Complex distribution and economic systems that have taken all this time to develop can disappear within months.

Our scientists say we've overshot our resource base, and the shortages that are killing people in the world's poorest countries will eventually reach all the way to the aisles of Costco. World population could be back to what it was in your time by 2050."

The head shrugs, or it would shrug if it had shoulders. The population of early nineteenth-century England no doubt seems plenty. What it really wants to know, I think, is what a Costco is.

"You'd like a Costco, Jeremy. It's a cornucopia, a big one in a cube-shaped cabinet exponentially bigger than the one built for your auto-icon. There's a lot of them, at least in the northern hemisphere.

"In a Costco, if you've got enough money you can have happiness beyond imagination. Anything you can imagine in the material world—and a bunch of things you can't—you can get at a Costco. Lots of people go to Costco, too, enough to be in the running for a greatest number back when the population was at your level. But theirs is a temporary abundance. Off the record, most of our scientists will say that climate and biosphere tipping points have been reached. Production curves that used to go up and up are plateauing, and some of them are going down. Crops are dying or shrinking as their climate zones move north. People are already leaving seacoasts due to the weather and high tides. When they're joined by the people they've sold their beach houses to, dry land is going to be more crowded and full of conflict than it's ever been.

"By the way, there seems to be a disjuncture between your hypothetical individual acting in benign self-interest and that same individual sharing a world where he has to compete, on a zero-sum basis, for food and clean water and living space. He still seems to act in self-interest. It's just not benign self-interest."

I realize that I'm talking to an imaginary head, one that looks even worse in my imagination than it did in its Internet photos. I'm hoping it doesn't ask me what a tipping point is, or a biosphere.

It doesn't seem to want to ask me anything. I decide it needs to go back in its box, and the box needs to go back in its Archaeology Department safe, until I have a first-year composition class again.

5

Thinking about survival on a planet where only the lucky or the ruthless survive is not new to me. I'm old enough to have been taught to duck and cover, which means I was introduced to nuclear war as part of my third-grade curriculum. For most of my life I've believed that I would die in a nuclear war. There's still a possibility that I'll die in a nuclear war, but I'm getting to the age now where nuclear war had better hurry itself up or I'm going to die of something else, and all that diving under desks in elementary school will be for naught.

If I don't die in a nuclear war, my mean old third-grade teacher, Mrs. Mac, who let us find our seats in early morning homeroom dark and then switched on the classroom lights to simulate the flash of a hydrogen weapon, is going to be revealed as the sadistic child abuser she was.

6

I can't believe that when I had a chance to tell Jeremy Bentham all about Utilitarianism's successes since his death, I left out national electrical grids, public health measures, and nuclear war. Especially nuclear war. If there's anything that brings up the concept of the greatest number, it's nuclear war and its more or less immediate symptom, human extinction. In algebraic terms, if the greatest number of humans equals y, for any value of y, y plus nuclear war equals zero. The concepts of happiness and suffering lose their heft when faced with zero, which doesn't seem like a big number at all until you get to it by subtracting all living humans.

Jeremy Bentham probably didn't intend it this way, but his concept of the greatest number has become an absolute. You can argue what happiness is and, Peter Singer notwithstanding, you can argue what right and wrong are. But you can't argue with the greatest number. It's just there, like Bentham's head, passive but difficult not to include in your deliberations.

Right now, our deliberations are of necessity focusing on how many people can fit on the planet and how many resources they will need for their happiness and what to do with the waste products of that happiness. Our efforts on behalf of our ever-growing numbers require as much farmland as possible growing as many crops as possible to feed as many people as possible, portions to be determined by dividing the total supply by the total number of people. Meat should not be eaten because—animal suffering aside—meat production is an inefficient use of people food. Of course, if a world of climate-imposed limits and extreme resource depletion means you can only feed a billion people no matter what you feed them, share-and-share-alike ethics dictate that everybody starves.

7

Peter Singer looks reasonable—and kind, sympathetic, and human, the kind of guy you'd like to have over for a vegan dinner—when he's decrying the commodification of sentient beings, consumption as a way of life, and the destruction of other peoples, cultures, and ecologies in the name of profit.

He's easy to agree with when he urges empathy and asceticism in their stead.

Empathy and asceticism are our only human weapons in a world where industrial civilization moves along, crushing mountains under its feet, melting the planet down and rendering everything it touches into product. It consumes and excretes and grows and emits a stench that we've come to accept as the air we breathe. Killing it would require that you deprive it of fossil fuels. Or that you forego empathy and asceticism and pound a sharpened stake into its heart, if you can find its heart.

But if that same civilization suddenly dies from an exponential feedback phenomenon, it's not good news for the greatest number of Americans, or even Idahoans. I worry about those people who will leave the cities and their suddenly empty supermarkets and come to Sawtooth Valley to look for food. Most of them won't be reading Peter Singer, but if their kids start dying of hunger, and all the local horses and cows and deer and elk and ground squirrels have been eaten, they're going to start wondering how many cans of pork and beans we've got in our crawl space.

I'm not comfortable depending on the empathy and asceticism of parents whose kids are starving. It sounds too much like an object lesson in the tyranny of the majority.

8

I don't know Peter Singer personally, but his writing has convinced me that he carries a grim missionary glee into his initial encounters with young people who start college thinking they have the ability to make the world a better place. He points out that they can do that if they're willing to give up half their money and decades of their lives, and change their diet to one that doesn't harm animals, and not have children, and work in a third-world clinic. He does this knowing that what he's asking is beyond a young American's usual capacity for sacrifice. But I assume he finds the occasional student willing to make that sacrifice, and I further assume that he then gets to work helping that person remake the world.

I've tried this sort of thing with my own students, but if he's done it once, Singer's more successful at it than I've ever been.

I once had a promising MFA student, a talented twenty-five-year-old woman who was writing a memoir. She came from a wealthy family and had traveled through five continents by the time she graduated from college. In spite of her youth, she had something to write about. She had touched the world, and not just on a touchscreen, and I was looking forward to helping her become a brilliant, fearless, and incisive writer.

The first story she gave me was about visiting an African refugee camp when she was sixteen. In that camp she had encountered a tiny six-year-old girl whose parents had both died of AIDS. The little girl knew enough English to say, "I have no mother. You be my mother. Please adopt me."

The experience caused my student a great deal of pain. As she looked at the little girl's pleading face, she felt terrible. "But what could I do?" she wrote. "I was sixteen, only ten years older than she was. I was going to college in two years. I couldn't be her mother." She left the refugee camp and the girl, but ten years later, she said, she still thinks about her. "You be my mother," went the last line of my student's story. "You be my mother."

I gave good advice to my student. I told her that you can jerk tears from your reader, but readers quickly develop a resistance to that sort of thing, and then they start looking critically at the moral stance of the writer.

"Of course you could have adopted her," I said, by way of explanation. "Lots of sixteen-year-olds are mothers or stepmothers. Some of them even make it through college. I'm sure the people running the refugee camp would have helped with the adoption process. Your parents probably could have been talked into it. You could have presented it as your way of saving the little girl's life, of keeping her from dying of AIDS or becoming a mother at thirteen or having to work as a prostitute.

"Think of how different things would be if you'd stepped out of the person you thought you could be and had become her mother and raised her. It's been ten years. She'd be the same age as you when you met her. She'd be a different person from the one she is. You'd be a different person from the one you are. Try writing a dialog between the person you are, who didn't adopt her, and the person you could have been, who did."

My next step, of course, was to reassure her that she didn't really have to go back to the refugee camp, find the girl, adopt her and her two or three children, and take them back to share a life of privilege in the United States.

"But you do have to be able to ask yourself what would have happened if you had. You also have to accept some amount of guilt if you're alive on this planet. You don't have to wallow in it, but as a writer you have to be able to experience it if you're going to understand the people you're writing for."

My advice made my student deeply uncomfortable. I had caused the sort of pain that Peter Singer seems to relish inflicting. Inflicting it didn't feel as good to me as I thought it would.

The work my student sent me for the rest of the semester was safe stuff, mostly sketches and stories that she had written for undergraduate workshops. When the semester was over, she dropped out of the MFA program and took off for Thailand, where her pain was no doubt tempered by the food, the beaches, and the smiles of a people who keep their refugee camps off-limits to most foreigners, because their whole country is engaged in creating the greatest happiness for the greatest number of tourists.

9

A book I've dusted off lately is Eric Hoffer's *The True Believer.* Hoffer published it in 1951, when the Nazis were fresh in humanity's memory.

I started rereading Hoffer about the time I decided that the majority of contemporary happiness-seekers might not be able to stand the pain of a dying world.

Hoffer analyzes mass movements and is concerned particularly with the effects such movements have on personhood. If Peter Singer presupposes an ethical and conscious individual inside every human being, Hoffer presupposes a slave in the same position, for whom consciousness represents just one more burden in life. Hoffer suggests that most people don't really like the task of creating a self and will give it up to any movement that offers them a feeling of belonging to something greater than themselves. It's faux-personhood for people who find real personhood an exercise in agony.

It would be difficult for any civilization to face resource depletion, an exploding population, and a lethal climate without resorting to a mass movement to hold things together. But America hasn't thus far seen the nationwide psychic contagions that allowed the Italian Fascists to administer castor oil to their once-dignified political opponents, the ss to slaughter Jews, Gypsies, and homosexuals, or the Chinese Red Guards to destroy Old Customs, Old Culture, Old Habits, Old Ideas, and Old People.

Hoffer notes that true believers will sacrifice themselves for what they see as the greater good. They will endure misery in the present for a someday utopia. And they will happily kill anyone who doesn't agree with their vision of what constitutes a future. If you don't see the connection between those people going to Costco in the twenty-first century just as they went to Nuremburg rallies in the twentieth, you haven't been reading Peter Singer.

10

On days when we could use a boost of civic cheer, however vicarious, Julie and I watch a livestream of the local evening news on KTVB, Boise's NBC affiliate. After the news, the livestream switches to a silent webcam of the Boise rush-hour traffic outside the KTVB studios. The traffic, a slow, almost placid river of light once the sun goes down, is a mass movement seemingly less harmful than most. Still, when Julie says, "We could be in one of those cars," it causes a spasm of claustrophobia.

Even though it's been a long time since I inflicted Peter Singer on undergraduates, he still shapes my sensibilities, and I can still see, in that stream of traffic, a terrific waste of resources, a headlong rush toward a world where people use food and fuel to go to and from jobs that support a global system of pain. Each one of those cars is a microcosm of the criminal.

Likely, Singer would say that the microcosm Julie and I have created is criminal as well. At times, it seems we've narrowed the definition of the greatest number to a privileged two, whose happiness deals death to the poor and helpless.

But what got us here to this small place wasn't a terribly restrictive definition of what constitutes a greatest number. It was the realization that humans, each of them attending to their own happiness, had inflicted unimaginable pain on every other species on the planet. That pain had intensified to the point where it was tearing great gaping holes in the web of life. It wasn't happening everywhere, which was why it was so hard to see it was happening. But we knew it would kill us all.

That was two decades ago. Julie and I didn't know how much time we had left. It was time to get the hell out of the zeitgeist. We've had far more time here, living well in this beautiful place, than we thought we would.

All the more reason not to invite Peter Singer to dinner. But if he showed up at the door hungry, we'd let him in. His presence wouldn't mean the end of our world, or the greatest pain for the greatest number, or a meal with pure guilt on the menu. Chances are, we'd have a language in common, and senses of right and wrong that weren't totally at odds with each other.

And maybe, by special arrangement with University College, we could wheel Jeremy Bentham's auto-icon up to the table as a non-eating member. Out of deference to Singer's sensibilities, we wouldn't bring the good wine out of the crawl space, but there's a few well-aged bottles of Two Buck Chuck down there, and they have the advantage of not needing a corkscrew. Add one of Julie's occasional vegan meals, and the four of us could become a tableau of happiness.

I doubt if the conversation would result in agreed-upon solutions to the current human predicament. Singer would argue for action in the face of misery, and Julie and I would caution against the misery of butterfly-effect unintended consequences.

Singer would argue against our selfish survivalism. We would reply that we're not expecting to survive.

Singer would suggest that moral imperatives aren't that hard for him to find in this world. We would say that since we concluded that our species was committing suicide, it's been hard for us to find any, outside of loving each other and treating the people we meet with such decency and kindness as we can.

Singer would say that you can't just withdraw to watch the world end. We would say that the importance of witnesses has been underestimated.

Bentham wouldn't say much at all. These issues aren't as urgent for him these days, given his lack of a head.

Where the four of us might find common ground is in imagining the kind of people we might be and what kind of world we might have created if long ago Jeremy Bentham had discovered that the greatest happiness lay in keeping the world and its creatures alive and whole. What sort of dialog could we have with those imaginary beings, who live in that imaginary place?

resort life

If the people who run the world's economy
spend all their time at ski resorts, it'll be
a while before they realize there's anything
wrong with the world economy.

1

For much of my life, I have taught people to write so they
could take difficult ideas and get them across to people who
didn't want to think about them. But the most difficult idea I
tried to get across to my students, the one *they* didn't want to
think about, was that they needed to learn to write.

Most of them thought they already knew how to write.
They'd gotten As on high school papers. They came to college
thinking they knew how to get yet more As on essays in my
composition class.

So when I assigned a reading about a woman who had
undergone enough cosmetic surgery to turn herself into a
popular toy, a lot of papers began, "You shouldn't have twenty-
nine plastic surgeries to turn yourself into a six-foot Barbie
doll because . . ."

When I assigned readings on young men of their parents'
generation fleeing to Canada to avoid going to Vietnam,
essays started out with, "We shouldn't have had a draft

because America is a free country and you weren't free if you had to go into the Army ..."

When I assigned Deborah Tannen's brilliant essay, "There is No Unmarked Woman," I read that, "Women shouldn't identify with their work once they have children because my mother quit her job when she had my brothers and me and she's happy just being a mom."

I would scribble Ds or Fs on these papers, which made my office a place of tears and anger. "What do you want me to say?" was a common question, as if learning to write was a matter of learning your catechism.

Other students assumed I was the sort of liberal academic that right-wing talk-show hosts railed against. I received well-written but dishonest papers that advocated transfers of wealth from rich to poor, from north to south, from former slave owners to former slaves, and so on. More Ds and Fs.

For a student used to getting As, an F is a catastrophe. In the case of a sincere effort to manipulate the professor, an F threatens the foundations of the universe.

Six weeks into a semester, when I wrote, "How to Get an A in this Class" on the board, I had everybody's attention. Here's what I wrote below that heading:

Stop obsessing about grades.

A writer should honor the world in all its terror and beauty. Never shrink the world to fit your own limitations and prejudices.

Use concrete nouns and action verbs. Put them in short sentences.

Tell the truth. Lying destroys brain cells.

Any paragraph longer than five sentences will confuse your audience and they'll stop reading. If they can't stop reading because reading your writing is their job, they'll give you Ds or Fs.

The next set of papers would be better. When you ask people to look around themselves and to write down what they see, they do see the world and begin to find words to describe it. When you ask people to look at their own limitations and prejudices, they begin to get glimpses of them in the shadows of their lives.

I tried to keep my students entertained. "Given the condition of the planet," I would say, "we'll probably all die on the same day. The difference between us will be that I've seen the Doors and Led Zeppelin and Jefferson Airplane in concert."

2

When I taught writing in an MFA program, I asked all my students to write a credo, a statement detailing why they wrote. It's a risky assignment. Sometimes when people sit down to discover the reasons they want to write, they can't find any. That's probably why I hadn't written one myself until a few years ago.

Even though one of my books is a why-to-write book, I still got into trouble when I wrote my own credo. Here are some excerpts:

A question I should have answered years ago: Why not just tell funny little stories to make people happy?

If I try to wake people to the condition of our world, which is best described as hospice-bound, I'll make them angry.

But a bunch of intelligent and mostly unexcitable people—scientists and journalists and philosophers—are pointing out a number of ways that humanity won't make it to the end of the century. Is anything else important enough to write about?

That question, which the minutiae of an academic job once insulated me from, seems to have gained urgency. I now have time to consider it rather than having it show up, smiling and friendly, stethoscope in hand, at my deathbed.

Also:

Can you trust your own perceptions in these matters?

If everything's so bad, why am I feeling so good?

These last two questions have the effect of making things a little inbred in the minds of the people who ask them. If you're in a spaceship, you shouldn't get too close to a black hole, and if you're writing a credo, you shouldn't consider questions that imply that reality is solipsism.

Better to put your faith in a real, human-scale world and try to be an honest and objective witness of it, even if that world is dying, even if you're the one holding the stethoscope and standing beside its deathbed, even if you're overcome with grief.

I don't know if anyone will be alive in a hundred years, except bacteria hanging out in hydrothermal caverns a mile beneath the earth's surface. If bacteria ever learn to read, I'd like them to know that in the last decades of human existence, a human looked around himself, thought about what he saw, and wrote down that thinking—dark existential jokes, mostly, which deep-biosphere bacteria prefer to all other forms of humor.

I ended with:

There's plenty to write about in this world, if you keep existentially funny and honestly grief-stricken about it.

If I'm a new student in my first writing class, and the professor writes "Existentially Funny and Honestly Grief-Stricken" on the board, I'm out of there, heading for an airport where I'll spend my tuition loan checks on tickets to someplace warm with a beach.

3

A writing professorship is a job you can define to your liking. It includes a tweed jacket, friendly questions from local reporters about holiday gift books, and the deep attention of students determined to discover the wellsprings of your vanity. These things were mine, and more. But I gave it up in return for a new title: Writer-at-Large for the College of Idaho, which mostly meant that I was out the College of Idaho's hair. The number of complaining students in the academic dean's office—outraged that their professor had just told them they would never see Jim Morrison in concert—went down when I left the campus.

Still, I retain some connections with the college. One of them is a friendship with the ski-team coach. Two winters ago he invited me to ski with the team as they trained at Sun Valley.

Sun Valley is the oldest and one of the most luxurious of American ski resorts. But its managers have realized that their mostly geriatric customers represent a high-mortality demographic. They're providing their facilities to college and high-school ski teams, hoping that these young people will become future paying customers. I went along as the future paying customers' unofficial assistant coach.

I wasn't much of a coach. For twenty years I've been on loose-fitting backcountry ski equipment. Ski racers ski on equipment designed for separating winners from losers by hundredths of a second. The students made fun of my skis, boots, and bindings when they weren't making fun of the old guy who replaced the gates when they knocked them down.

But when I got on the gondola at the bottom of the mountain, people in Sun Valley Company livery took my skis, put them in the ski rack, and ushered me to my seat. At the top they handed my skis back and asked if I needed help putting them on.

Somewhere during my second gondola ride, I realized that if the people who run the world's economy spend their time at ski resorts, it will be a while before they realize anything's wrong with the world economy. They'll be a hundred feet off the ground in a gondola when the electricity goes. Only hours later, when it's dark and nobody has rescued them, will they realize the only bubble left is the one they're sitting in, swaying back and forth in a cold wind.

I trusted the electrical grid enough to ride the gondola for a few days. When a high-speed lift takes you to the top of a mountain, and that mountain is covered with artificial snow groomed to millimeter tolerances, you can, for brief moments, imagine you're an Olympic racer—at least until your legs give out halfway down the mountain.

In the evenings I ate with the ski team. I asked them what they planned to do after they graduated and how they were paying for college.

They had taken out loans, or their parents had. They didn't know what they were going to do after graduation. The question scared them.

Besides race training, these young people spent their week at Sun Valley skating, bowling, and swimming in the Lodge pool. They slept in luxurious condos, as befitted future paying customers.

I decided that in their hearts, these student-athletes imagined their future the same way Sun Valley Company did. In twenty years they would be aging champions with ski-racer children. They would ski through long sunny days, compete in masters' races, drink fine wines and eat in high-end restaurants, then go back to cathedral-sized homes and sleep the sleep of the just before getting up and doing it all again. Sun Valley is, at present, full of geriatric athletes who are proving that dream is possible.

And yet, that won't happen for these students. In the world they will graduate into, the old social contract—work hard, save your money, pay your bills—has been replaced by a new one that says borrow your money, work hard, and die in how-did-I-get-here debt to people who didn't work hard but did give you loans.

Some of them won't believe in global warming while there's still snow to ski on. But even they can see we're destroying what's left of a beautiful world in our haste to turn it all into commodity. We're heading for eight billion humans on the planet. Anyone with a pocket calculator can determine we haven't got room or resources to do what we've been doing for yet another generation.

What are you going to do after graduation? The question scares me, too, and I'm about to turn seventy years old.

4

As a professor teaching eighteen- to twenty-two-year-olds, I necessarily became a student of narcissism, which I define as not knowing where your boundaries end and the world begins. It's not always a bad thing, if you can admit that other people have boundary problems too, especially when you trample on their boundaries. Psychologists call narcissism that's been moderated by empathy *healthy* narcissism.

Writing itself is an attempt to expand your boundaries, a

demand that people stop what they're doing and pay attention because you know something they need to know. It helps if you've figured out something they really do need to know, like a future that isn't going to be anywhere near what they think it will be.

Healthy narcissism or not, most people, when they're told about something that alters what they expect out of life, will experience their boundaries being violated. They will shut it out of their minds.

When I told my students that there were too many people on the planet? It didn't cause anyone not to make babies. When I told them the planet's atmosphere was a chaotic system, and when you change the composition of a chaotic system the weather can turn lethal? That didn't stop them from preparing for jobs in the shale-fracking industry. When I told them that without a way to redistribute wealth, capital would accumulate in stagnant, algae-choked pools and destroy our economic system? That didn't keep them from going deep into debt to pay for college and from signing up for thirty-year mortgages a year into their first job.

After being ignored on life-and-death matters, I began to think about *un*healthy narcissism, which is when you see other people as nothing but extensions of yourself. You, however incomplete you might be, become the world and everybody in it.

This sounds improbable but becomes familiar territory when I say that many of my students saw professors as minor character actors in the miniseries they were starring in. Professors had their costumes and their quirky ways, but we had only bit parts until we gave them a D or an F. Then we became minor villains, written out of the script by the next semester's episode.

The stories these students saw themselves in were mostly

harmless to others, even their professors. But they were deeply harmful to the people who made them up. Their stories were so tacky and predictable that they reduced their world to a third-rate stage set, and their lives to fourth-rate soap operas.

Occasionally my students would wake up in the middle of the drama. They would say, "I've spent my life studying so I can get good grades so I can get into a good college so I can get into a good grad school so I can get a good job and have a good career and have a good marriage and good kids and graduate to a good retirement community until I'm taken to a good nursing home to die in the middle of morphine hallucinations."

"Only if your good college loans are paid off," I would tell them. "Otherwise, no morphine for you."

5

But most students never woke up, and they defended their stories as though they were defending human existence itself. That's the trouble with narcissism: start seeing the world as an extension of yourself, and the world becomes fragile, temporary, wounded by your wounds, and ended by your physical or philosophical death.

6

Philosophical death (by neglect) is a concept that comes to us from the philosopher Bertrand Russell. He used to tell a story about a philosophically dead rooster, who said, "Every day my farmer comes with food and water. He's a good guy. He cleans my coop, makes sure I have an adequate supply of hens, protects me from the foxes I glimpse on the other side of the wire, and he does all these things out of gratitude for my glorious crowing that serves to start the day."

Russell says that one day the farmer comes to the coop with an axe, and that's the day the rooster decides he needs philosophy after all.

7

I was born in Sun Valley in 1950. The Sun Valley Resort had the best hospital in the area, on the third floor of the Lodge, a holdover from the time the entire resort had been a Navy hospital during World War II. My mother worked there as a nurse before and after I was born.

When I was six my father started driving ski buses at the resort. Because I was an employee kid, I skied free. My skis and poles and boots were secondhand, and I received no instruction, but mileage counts in skiing. By the time I was in high school I was a good skier.

By age seventeen I was a Sun Valley ski patrolman. I tobogganed people with broken legs and torn knees down to ambulances. I'd ride with them to the emergency room. I discovered that people in shock often believe they're seeing things clearly for the first time in their lives. It made me wonder what they thought they had been seeing before they were injured.

I became an even better skier. Ski reps gave me equipment. I could dance through a field of moguls, touching down on every second or third one. Paying customers cheered me on from the lifts. I saw my life as an example of what the paying customers would do if they only had the time.

At age twenty-two I became the mountain manager for Sun Valley's bunny hill and entered into Sun Valley Company's executive training program.

At management meetings with the president of the company, I was introduced to the idea that running a ski mountain is a form of agriculture. At night the fields were groomed for a new crop of skiers. Fresh feed had to be brought to the mountain restaurants, injured livestock had to be carted away, stock driveways had to be maintained, and predators—people sneaking onto the lifts without tickets or who skied too fast—had to be eliminated.

At first, I enjoyed being a farmer. There were worse things than to be an athletic twenty-two-year-old executive-in-training at a ski resort during the time America was enjoying the fevered finances of a new war economy. Unlimited wealth was in the air. People who had made fortunes producing Agent Orange and napalm and metal and epoxy composites for military aircraft built giant houses below the ski slopes, satisfied that they had contributed enough to society to retire. Some of them gave me money to ski with them on my days off.

But narcissism—even when it's your own—quickly wears thin, no matter how self-indulgent your skills allow you to be. I began to see my life as a tedious slideshow of other people's leisure time. At the end of that season, I backed out of the training program and asked for my old job back as an ordinary ski patrolman.

When I got back in the patrol shack, the people I worked with treated me with contempt. I had rejected a step up in the system. They saw me as a slacker, or crazy, or both. I lasted the season and then found a job as a teacher, where the steps up were more numerous, and the work a little less like farming.

But not much less. It has not escaped my notice that I tend to quit jobs when I start glimpsing the shimmering outlines of the inhuman structure that I'm caught in.

8

I live in a country whose highest court has said that corporations are people.

The court is right. Corporations are people. They want to feed and grow and have children and party hard. Sometimes they become addicts or go insane.

But even sane corporations are hard to live with. Corporations treat their employees—even their CEOs—as genetically modifiable organisms, or profit centers, or both. Corporations go bankrupt to get out of pension obligations to their retired employees. They move plants to countries with slave labor.

Corporations are people, but they're not nice people.

In Hanoi, visiting the Temple of Literature, I ran into another American tourist, one working for Monsanto in Beijing. He told me that his team was trying to figure out how Monsanto could produce as much food in the next fifty years as all the food humans have produced in the last seven thousand. "If we don't," he said, "billions of people will starve."

"What will you have to do?" I asked.

"Turn the world into a farm," he said.

I don't think he understood how much violence against the world and its creatures he was talking about. One of my more dismal realizations is that corporations have figured out that they need to be people, but they have no need for anybody else to be people.

9

Here's what I told my writing students, late in the semester: "In an infinite universe, we each occupy a point. It's not much, but it's our point, and we possess it entirely, and it us. No matter where we go, it traps us in the dead center of all we can see."

"If that's so," they asked, "how can you possibly get through to people who haven't seen what you've seen? How do you take difficult ideas and get them across to people who don't want to think about them?"

I said, "With great effort and care you learn the language of truth. Then you can sneak through their defenses with an image, a story, or just a word of grief or joy.

"One true thing," I said. "Get it across to another human being, anytime in your life. I'll give you a retroactive A."

10

Since corporations are so much bigger than humans, it's possible for us to feed off their excretions, like a little sweat bee, snug and warm in an adipose fold, going along for a ride not possible under our own power.

Every summer the Sun Valley Company hosts a symphony orchestra. The orchestra plays on the leafy and nitrogen-green grounds of the resort, in a huge copper-roofed amphitheater made of big blocks of travertine. Sun Valley Music Festival musicians come from all over the planet. A few summers ago, Julie and I drove down to hear them perform Tchaikovsky's speedy Opus 35 in D major.

Vadim Gluzman, one of the world's best violinists, did the honors, playing the 1690 Stradivarius that had belonged to Tchaikovsky's mentor. It was the instrument the work had been written for.

We were on the lawn above the amphitheater with a picnic and a bottle of good wine, listening to the concert through speakers and watching it on a theater-sized screen. But during the last two movements I walked to the top row of seats, knelt down, and watched Gluzman through binoculars. I gave up any ambitions to play the violin.

Cultural critics claim that Tchaikovsky's concerto is a high point of civilization. If so, Gluzman's performance kicked civilization to a new peak, at least for a half hour in North America in the early part of the twenty-first century.

It was a warm afternoon. As happy people came streaming out of the amphitheater, Julie and I stayed in our chairs. We were in no hurry. The concert traffic would take a half hour to clear, and we still had chocolate left.

I began to think it was odd that I had been born here and was still here, only a hundred yards away from the room I had been born in. I had thought I'd make it further in life.

Then I thought there were worse places to end up than in a community of civic-minded millionaires and billionaires, listening to an orchestra of the world's best musicians. There were worse years to have been born than 1950, and worse skies to live under than the ones of central Idaho.

I should have stopped thinking right there. But I noticed that many of the couples attending the concert consisted of well-preserved and purposeful women leading confused old men to and from their seats. It's what happens when you pair young women with older men, then add some decades. My mind jumped ahead to hanging up the skis, the bypass, and the moment when you start looking for the rotary dial on the cell phone.

My mind went further, into the amphitheater. Travertine affects me like a drug. Small doses make me think of pastoral follies—the fake Roman ruins built on English estates in the nineteenth century.

But I was gazing into a massive travertine overdose. I saw, in the roof's skeletal understructure, a time when the civilization that had built it had become dust.

Thieves had stripped the roof of its copper. The dressing rooms on either side of the stage had become holding pens for the reluctant stars of blood rituals.

I suddenly wanted the Sun Valley Music Festival to arrange a midnight performance of *Carmina Burana*, with the Mormon Tabernacle Choir on risers at the back of the stage. The amphitheater would be lit by flickering torches. The Choir would be amplified by high-dose amphetamines. Human sacrifices during the finale would ensure a bountiful potato harvest.

The amphitheater emptied. Julie got a purposeful look on her face and said it was time for us to go. It took a moment to understand that she wasn't talking about baby boomers.

I took our wine bottle to the recycling bin. I helped Julie fold up our chairs and gather the remains of our picnic. Then the two of us walked slowly back to our car, which sat by itself in the emptied parking lot.

We walked in golden slanted sunlight. There was no wind. We were glad to be in the moment, and reluctant to think that we might ever have to leave it.

the unconscious
and the dead

*The best classes always have
somebody dying in them.*

1

I had titled the course *The Unconscious as Literature*.

No matter that I didn't know what I was talking about.
Any time you talk about the unconscious you can't know what
you're talking about. That's why it's called the unconscious.

"What I want from you by the end of the semester," I told
my students on the first day of class, "is an understanding that
it's not what you know, but what you don't know that will
determine your life.

"At this point, you no doubt think you are conscious
beings. You're dead wrong. Consciousness is possible only
after decades of being honest with yourself followed by more
decades of honest assessment of the world. Even then, it's
mostly illusion.

"Your consciousness won't pick the person you marry. It
won't choose what kind of sex you have and how often. It won't
decide if you have children, or if you abuse drugs and alcohol.
It won't determine how you talk to your parents, or if you'll
graduate. It's your *un*conscious that will preside over these
things, as well as what music you dance to, what corporation

you work for if you're lucky enough to get a job, and whether or not you plagiarize the paper you write for this class."

Not good news for my students, at least if they had believed me. Most of them were certain that by going to college they had achieved freedom—and its necessary component, consciousness—for the first time in their lives. But I had been teaching undergraduates for fifteen years and had plenty of evidence that none of my students—or colleagues, for that matter—had made the big decisions of their life from a place of much awareness.

I had taught people who had married abusers after childhoods with abusive parents. Some of my former students had changed genders after being heterosexually married for ten years. One had gone into the hospital for an appendectomy and come out with a new baby.

I had taught people who worshipped money when they called themselves devout Christians. Others had gone into teaching because they had high needs for control, into politics because they deep down wanted to hurt people, or into medicine because they loved sickness rather than health.

I also had a photocopied stack of plagiarized papers in my office. I had handed back the originals to their purported authors, saying, "You're way smarter than I thought you were. You get an A. That's got to feel good."

I thought it was a clever way of shocking people into an awareness of their own destructive impulses while I gave vent to a few of mine.

I didn't shock anybody into anything. Over my career I watched as self-awareness arrived, usually too late to do any good. I knew people who had died in Afghanistan or Iraq because of subliminal family expectations, or who had overdosed on drugs that allowed a glimpse of a world they yearned for but couldn't live in, or who had killed themselves for love or the lack of it. People who had gone deeply into debt for medical degrees quit medicine and drove trucks or opened bakeries. People struggling through grad school became parents when they didn't want children and couldn't afford them. People got depressed or sick when choices they hadn't made began to require more of their time and energy than the choices they had. Highly intelligent and literate colleagues smoked and drank and ate themselves to death.

Witnessing these things made me think that self-awareness requires constant maintenance. If you don't continually work on becoming ever more aware, parts of the person you think of as you—maybe all of the you that you think of as you— will sink into a dream not too far up the continuum from death. A disturbing corollary to this idea is that if you try to go in the opposite direction, your unconscious will be exposed to the light, and it doesn't like the light.

"We will start with a few scenarios," I told the class. "One presumes that the unconscious is just blind impulse from the parts of your brain inherited from fish and reptiles, something to be controlled, if possible, by reason, so you can live as free and thinking beings instead of just eating and shitting, spawning and dying. Another envisions the unconscious as an alien entity in your skull, one that wants to keep on living its unexamined life even at the expense of destroying your awareness. Yet another is that the unconscious is the underworld, alive and stirring beneath your feet, full of paths not taken, unborn selves, unexpressed yearnings, and forbidden thoughts."

2

A student's hand went up. It belonged to Charley, who had been in one of my classes already. I'd given him an A, not because he was a plagiarist, but because every time I read one of his papers, I realized he was more intelligent than I'd thought he was, and I'd decided he was more intelligent than I was to begin with. He didn't have to be told that free will was illusion, for one thing.

Charley had been diagnosed with soft-tissue sarcoma when he was seventeen. Now he was twenty-two, having lived four years longer than he had been told he would, mostly because every time a tumor showed up in his CAT scans, his doctors cut it out.

He was a shadow of his former self. He was missing lymph glands, chunks of muscle, his hair, and portions of both lungs—those were just the parts I knew about. His highest ambition was to live long enough to graduate, but over the semester break he had sat at a big table with his doctors and nurses, his physical therapist, the hospital chaplain, and a hospice worker. They told him he wasn't going to make it.

"I have a scenario for you," Charley said to all of us. "I've got three months to live. It's a lousy way to get out of a final. I'd appreciate it if you'd make this class the best class I've ever had."

We considered his words in silence. The classroom looked the same, but the walls, the furniture, and the language cast shadows that hadn't been there before. Even Charley, as a shadow, cast a shadow. He still had to take a final, for one thing. Just not my final.

I spent the rest of the class going over the reading list. I had doubts that the class would be the best class of Charley's life, but I thanked him anyway for giving us a head start on dealing with the unconscious.

3

Charley, dead for over a decade, has lately been on my mind. He doesn't visit me in dreams, but he's started to speak to me when I sit out on my deck with a cup of coffee.

For a long time I didn't think I could talk to him because he's dead. That has proven less of a barrier than I expected on these warm and smoky mornings of fire season. Charley and I have a dialog of sorts, although he won't answer any questions about where he is now.

Also, he issues disclaimers: "If there's any part of me left in your world," he says, "if I'm not just a hallucinatory caffeine overdose, I still doubt that what I have to say will be of interest to you. You're alive. I'm dead. Death rearranges priorities."

"That's why it was so good to have you in class," I say. "We couldn't watch you taking notes for an exam you'd never take and not be a little more thoughtful about what we were talking about. We thought you were seeing something we weren't."

"The best classes always have somebody dying in them," he says.

"As long as it's not the professor," I say.

He grins. I suddenly realize he has no lips. "Your turn's coming."

"After your chair was empty," I say, "the class had a game: What Would Charley Say? It fit well with the other game we played: I Know What You're Really Saying and Why You're Really Saying It."

4

One of the books I assigned was Vladimir Nabokov's *Lolita*. It illustrates how humans confuse unconscious imperatives with conscious decisions. Fifty-five-year-old Humbert Humbert, the novel's narrator, mistakes twelve-year-old Lolita for a mythical being wonderfully inserted into his gray existence, when in reality she's a little girl whose nascent self cannot bear his gaze, much less his touch. He kidnaps her anyway and takes her on a motel-to-motel road trip across America, where his possessive lust and tacky fear of growing old drags her from semi-divine nymphhood into an ugly and claustrophobic middle age.

By the end of the novel, Humbert Humbert is in jail, dying, but Lolita has it worse. Once she existed in unthinking beauty and timeless grace, but she's become an ordinary housewife—Nabokov's word for her is slattern—forever exiled from the soft-lit green and gold and endlessly renewed world that nymphs inhabit, forever unable to connect with the eternal spark that once animated her. It's hard not to see Lolita's transformation as a murder.

Humbert Humbert can't enter Lolita's pristine and youthful world, which is what he unconsciously wants to do. Instead he pulls her into his own decaying life. The lesson is clear: touch a goddess, and she'll turn into rotten flesh in your arms.

The old idea that humans die when they see or touch a god is exactly wrong. No god can experience the human touch and live.

"But there's another way to look at this," I told the class, which at that point still included Charley. "Humbert Humbert sees Lolita as a metaphor that counters his fear of aging. But she's a literal human being. You don't turn human beings into metaphors unless you want to wreck them."

Charley spoke up: "I'm not a human being. I've been turned into a metaphor."

Other students immediately protested that of course Charley was a human being. He shrugged and said he would explain in his paper for the class. He sent it to me from his hospital bed. It was seventy-one pages. He apologized for not finishing it.

He began by describing his return from anesthesia after yet another operation:

Slowly I piece together what has been done to my body. An IV in my right arm, an IV in my neck, an arterial in my left arm, a catheter in my penis, an epidural catheter in my spine, two tubes (one anterior, one posterior) going in between my ribs, a blood pressure cuff that turns on every ten minutes, six EKG probes on my chest hooked to a monitor, a pulse oximeter measuring blood oxygen saturation on my right pinkie, an oxygen line in my nose, and two bags around my calves that inflate and deflate to keep fluid from pooling in my lower extremities.

The bad pain is four hours away. While I'm still floating, I'll tell you about this place—the ICU—and Lucretia, my ICU nurse.

Lucretia is a high-strung, by-the-book bitch who has never gotten over the fact that she's not a doctor.

Lucretia knows me as "twenty-one-year-old male undifferentiated sarcoma, post-operative right lower lobectomy for chest metastases." But she calls me Thoracotomy Bed Two, for short.

Lucretia doesn't like me. It's not that Thoracotomy Bed Two is a bad person. But Lucretia has never taken care of a thoracotomy that wants to be a person before. Lucretia is [usually] in charge of bypassers and renal failures, who apparently don't care about being persons.

Lucretia doesn't like having Thoracotomy Bed Two for another reason—I probably won't die during her shift. She wants to have Angioplasty Bed Six, so she can get the crash cart out when he codes in five hours.

Lucretia needs a fix, and unless my heart stops, she's
won't get it.

I hate Lucretia. But when the pain comes, I'm nice to
her. She has the key to the narcotics drawer.

That's what Charley wrote after the last surgery of his life.
Pity Lucretia. Pity any nurse or doctor who has a patient
who understands the violence that's been done to him and
who has realized how much of that violence is unconscious.

The rest of Charley's essay covers a wide range of his
dying experience, but if I had to sum it up, I'd say that it's the
account of an aware human being trying to stay aware in the
face of malignancies—his cancer, and the medical system it's
condemned him to, and that system's personnel, just doing
their jobs.

5

Does our civilization have an unconscious? That was the
question I asked my students after Charley left us halfway
through *The Unconscious as Literature*. We had seen a collection of authors struggle to explain what the unconscious was
and fail most of the time.

"The unconscious isn't only a dusty subterranean tomb
full of mystical statues," I said from the lectern. "It isn't just
burned fragments of parchment entombed in the Mediterranean mud off Alexandria. It isn't the ancient gods swimming
under the surface of contemporary religions and occasionally
sucking down a human sacrifice or two."

It had not been a scientific reading list.

But every one of my students asserted that our civilization
did have an unconscious. They went further. Their families
had an unconscious. The college had an unconscious. The

local police department had an unconscious. The companies they were planning on interning for that summer had an unconscious, and they wanted to know what they could about it before their interviews.

By that time my students were seeing the unconscious in the toasted tortillas on their plates in the dining hall.

"Often enough," I said, when it appeared they were getting carried away, "the unconscious is simply a kind of malignant stupidity. You can find it anywhere.

"Look at the First World War, and the Second. Look at the nuclear arms race, which occurred after, not before, Hiroshima and Nagasaki had shown what nuclear weapons could do to cities and the people in them.

"The genocides come to mind: the American Indians, the Armenians, the Ukrainians, the Jews, the Bosnians and Rwandans, Congolese, and Syrians, to name just a few—where some essential consciousness in the killers had to fade away before they could do what they did to their neighbors. The crazed courtroom faces of the old dictators tell us that the conscious mind cannot face what the unconscious has done."

Charley's empty chair had *me* carried away. "Malignant stupidity is implicit in the growth of capitalism, at least if you graph capitalism's projected expansion over the next fifty years and imagine what will be left of our green and gold world after it's run through capitalism's rendering machine.

"It's in continued population growth—the explosion followed by the crash, followed by further crashes as the environmental destruction of the original overshoot hits home.

"When you view the unconscious like this, it's like glimpsing a crazed reptile grin peeking from a broken window in a ruined city."

Back on the deck, I ask Charley, "How long have we got? I've got friends with grandchildren."

"How long?" he asks. "Time really isn't an issue from my standpoint. Maybe you should go back over what you said in class. Check your notes."

In my office I find a faded folder labeled *Unconscious Lit* and take it back to the deck.

I read,

> The unconscious isn't aware of time. If it's a place, time doesn't exist there. If it's just the non-neocortex parts of the brain, it has no more concept of the future than cows calmly walking up the curved ramp of a well-designed slaughterhouse.
>
> That brings up a dilemma. Is time something that exists independently of consciousness, and consciousness just makes us aware of it? Or is time just the illusory by-product of consciousness, and every minute of this class is a false division of eternity? Theologians, theoretical physicists, and the people in charge of nuclear waste storage would like to know.

"Pretty insensitive words to say to a kid who's been told he's got weeks to live," Charley says. "I had nightmares about that curved ramp in the slaughterhouse."

6

Also on the class reading list was an essay from the 1980s by the plain-spoken Jungian Michael Ventura, titled "Cities of the Psyche." The essay notes an uncanny similarity between satellite photos of suburbs and photomicrographs of computer chips.

Ventura suggests that in each case we're building structures that turn the unconscious into flesh—we don't consciously design chip architecture, we just figure out ways to make a chip smaller, cooler, more compact, and better at manipulating ones and zeroes.

We don't consciously design suburbs from the air, either. We just try to satisfy criteria for real-estate profits, master bathrooms, commuting, lawn care, pizza delivery, backyard barbeques, cocktail parties, baseball, soccer, and adultery.

Ignore the scale, and computer chips and cities look identical. Ventura has the idea that something is using humanity as a tool to create itself. Something beyond the human is making us build structures too small or too big for humans. It can't all be due to body-image disorders.

So we have the pyramids of the Egyptians and the Maya, echoing cathedrals all over medieval Europe, inhumanly rational skyscrapers with inhumanly empty nighttime streets below them, great soulless hospitals named after saints, missiles named after gods, musical instruments shaped like women, guns shaped like men. Toward the end of *The Unconscious as Literature* we had begun compulsively making these connections, seeing the campus clock tower as homage to the god Priapus, our college cheerleaders as sacrificial virgins to the same god, and the Middle East–bound ROTC students as sacrifices to the nasty old god Moloch, who promised ever increasing prosperity in exchange for the children.

One connection I deliberately didn't mention was the shady and unproveable hypothesis that cancer was a product of the unconscious. In that direction lay a scapegoat-the-cancer-victim madness, and I didn't want to go there while Charley was still with us.

Charley went there for me, saying, "Having cancer is like having all the scenarios of the unconscious hit you at once.

"In the basement of my hospital is a refrigerator," he went on. "In it is a petri dish full of cancer cells. It's got my name on it. There's a bunch of petri dishes with it. All of them have names on them. Some of those names belong to people who used to be my friends, but they died.

"What's in that petri dish will outlive me. It will outlive you, too, unless someone forgets to feed it."

Despite his total lack of hair and the divots in his physique, Charley was a good-looking guy. He had girlfriends he had met at Camp Rainbow Gold, the wilderness camp for cancer survivors where he volunteered every summer. The problem was that Charley's girlfriends all had their own petri dishes in the refrigerator.

Charley said, "You never know if you have cancer or cancer has you. My doctors say that my cancer is cells that should have died out before I was born but didn't. They were here first."

7

No doubt Charley's cancer cells, even now sitting in the hospital basement along with all their fellow campers—Camp Rainbow Gold for the neoplastic set—consider themselves perfectly conscious and focused on the business at hand, which is to divide and grow and keep dividing as long as somebody's supplying nutrients. They might look unconscious from the outside, but they wouldn't agree, thank you very much. They've got all the consciousness they need for the job they're doing.

We have to look at things from Charley's standpoint to realize his cancer cells are insensate entities in an underground refrigerator, kept alive for research purposes, dependent on human beings who are trying to figure out ways to kill them in vivo. Humans are part of the unconscious of every cancer cell. They're not aware of us, although they might have an uneasy feeling that something out there beyond the petri dish doesn't mean them well.

How do you get from the consciousness of a cancer cell to the much greater consciousness of Charley, who has a wider understanding of the petri dish and its nutrients?

8

We have become a depressingly aged and unfulfilled civilization, as civilizations go. Time has caught up with us. Where once we were full of promise and lust for life, we are now sticking to the known and the comfortable. In financial terms, we're living on interest rather than producing. In agricultural terms, we're eating the seed corn. In ecological terms, we're parasitic.

We've begun to feed on our young, not just through college loans and home mortgages and the military campaigns of a tottering empire, but also in our fascination with their quick energy and apparent immortality. Latter-day vampirism has emerged as wealthy baby boomers transfuse the blood of debt-serf millennials into their veins.

Even the most benign-spirited parents hold their children close, keeping them living at home far beyond the time when they should leave, limiting their independence and their options and networking them into jobs and careers that will fence in their horizons before they're thirty.

The diagnosis has come down, and it's not benign. Malignancies of our civilization—the waste of resources, a commitment to endless growth in a finite world, an inequality that dehumanizes both rich and poor, the lethal junk that floats in our oceans, to name only a few—these things should have died out before our civilization was born, and maybe if we had worked at becoming aware of their consequences they would have. But we stayed unconscious, and they stayed alive, and now they and their metastases are killing the world.

They haven't killed it yet. But give them time. Better yet, take time away and put eternity in its place.

In eternity, all exponential curves go vertical. Unintended consequences dance out into the open for everyone to see. The slow buildup of greenhouse gases in our atmosphere becomes lethal when seen through the lens of eternity. So does the best-designed nuclear power plant. In eternity, the four or five big nuclear accidents that the world has seen in eighty years become twelve or fifteen hundred in the twenty-four-thousand-year half-life of plutonium. And that's not even a little bit of eternity.

In eternity, longevity becomes dementia. Oilfields go dry. Oceans warm and turn to acid. Effective antibiotics last for relative nanoseconds. Pesticides become nutrients for weeds. Species wink into and out of existence. Deserts crawl north across continents. Corporations and countries are born, grow, wither, and die. Civilizations do the same. Species die. Suns expand into the orbits of their planets.

As Charley might say, there are as many endings as beginnings in the big scheme of things.

9

I deliver Charley a cup of coffee on the deck. We make the sad discovery that he's not solid enough to pick it up. "That's okay," I say. "I'll drink it."

"I miss coffee," he says.

"I'd die without it," I say.

"Not funny."

"Tell me," I say. "Does consciousness exist after death?"

"Sure," he says. "But there's general agreement that it doesn't exist before death."

If, by the end of *The Unconscious as Literature*, we had little idea of what the unconscious was, my students at least knew how to recognize the signs of it in their lives. They began to look critically at their relationships and to say, to people they once thought they would marry, "I know what you're really saying when you say that."

Other students, who previously couldn't stand each other, fell in love—because they could finally see what the other was really saying when they said what they said, and even if it wasn't nice, it was true, and once you're aware of the unconscious, true is always preferable to nice. Not that they don't sometimes go together.

Students began to do their own laundry rather than face the nuances attendant to taking it home for Mom to wash on weekends. They began to talk to their grandparents about their parents, learning embarrassing family secrets. They began to look critically at their professors, even when I discouraged that sort of thing.

In short, because they gained a perspective on the unconscious, the students began to show the sort of aware maturity that small liberal-arts colleges point to when they try to justify tuition increases. Some of this new perspective was due to me, some of it was due to the readings, but much of it was due to Charley and his mortality-aware ability to say what he really meant at the time he was saying it.

Over my career, most of my good classes did have somebody who was dying in them, whether the class and I knew it or not. Whether it was an actual physical dying or a *Lolita*-style dying didn't matter as much as the fact that in each of those classrooms, death was transformed from an abstract idea into something that gave daily life heft and substance.

These days it's the impending death of our civilization that is endowing what remains of our lives with heft and substance, and the classroom is the Earth. It's time to play one more game of What Would Charley Say.

"Here's what I'd say," says Charley, trying and failing again to pick up his coffee. "It's the things that humans do know, rather than the things they don't know, that are determining the fate of the planet."

"You mean we're not lemmings, unconsciously diving off a cliff?"

"You're lemmings diving off a cliff," he says.

Then he says, "You used to tell us that one way of approaching the unconscious was to realize it was out to get us. But the unconscious is just the world. If you want to make any part of it conscious, take it seriously and look at it honestly. That's all consciousness is: taking things seriously and not lying to yourself.

"If you think of it that way, consciousness doesn't come from the self. It comes from outside the self. It always was outside of the self, in plain sight. The self just has to stop defending against it."

Then he mutters, "I really miss coffee," and disappears into the underworld.

I'm all alone in the sunshine, and it's getting warm out here and I'm without sunscreen in a world where the ozone layer is still delicate despite our best efforts. That question I was going to ask Charley—about how consciousness can exist in a place where time doesn't—will have to wait.

I pick up Charley's full coffee cup and look up at the mountains. In the past they've had snow on them this time of year, but it melted fast this spring. Only small patches of white mark the north-slope gullies. Most of the trees below them are beetle-killed. There's smoke from seven hundred thousand acres of nearby burning forest in the air, and a layer of wood ash has drifted onto the deck.

It's not too much to say that we humans have become the Humbert Humbert of species, and the green world we feed on has become our Lolita.

But in my small part of that world, autumn will come, bringing a paradoxical renewal. The air will clear and cool, and if the fire hasn't made it to the deck and the house, I'll still look out on a beautiful if blackened horizon.

At that moment I'll know that gazing out on a burnt-over world brings beauty into being. I'll know that having Charley in my class made me a better professor. I'll know that Lucretia, the smiling keeper of Charley's narcotics supply, is more real when she's got a patient in pain. I'll know that Lolita might have become a slattern even without Humbert Humbert in her life, because it's in the nature of nymphettes to age and thicken, but it still would have been better if he had left her alone.

There is no class for whom to turn these statements into questions, and at this stage of retirement I'm glad of that. Still, there is much to be said for asking questions that can be answered by looking carefully and without prejudice at the world, especially if the answers then look like they were there all along.

We could actively observe as a civilization and discover that we know more about our problems than we think we do. We might even find solutions enough to save ourselves from the future that haunts us.

But we've reserved our questions of policy for the unconscious, forgetting that the unconscious is an endless and eternal and infinitely complex set of circumstances that takes things only as seriously as it has to. It doesn't have to solve our problems. Unlike consciousness, it doesn't have to care, and it doesn't have to grieve. Common sense says that it's stopped taking humanity and its little sparks of consciousness seriously.

Against that indifference I can only sit and talk with Charley on these delicate, orange-lit mornings on my deck, with coffee. I realize we won't save civilization. But we might save what's left of Charley until fire season comes around again, and that will be something in the face of nothing, and that is enough for now.

the way we
live now, again

*Maybe we don't need dementia metaphors
to explain what's going on in the world.*

1

The world outside our windows is bright white in January
and a patchwork of lush greens in June. The air is clear except
during wildfire season. There's gas in our vehicles and electricity in our outlets. Our computers still function as portals to
the Internet. UPS and FedEx deliver to our door. The Social
Security Administration, my TIAA annuities, and Julie's job
still deposit money in our accounts every month. Now and
then I get a check from someone willing to pay me for what
I write.

We live under a wide and gifting sky, which stretches to
the ragged horizons of the valley. The sunsets are good, even
when transformed into gauzy, gaudy neon by burning forests
or Chinese coal plants. Sunrises, heralding a new day, are even
better. Full moons are good, even when they're a fiery orange.
Stars are good. On cloudless and smokeless nights the Milky
Way looks like bright dust hovering next to the dark shapes of
the peaks.

The experience is a bit giddy when you realize you're looking down, not up. From our deck we watch meteor showers

rise toward us in August and December, although we don't last long outside in December.

Somewhere in those depths lurk black holes. We haven't yet fallen into one. At least I don't think so. It's hard to tell, when you're approaching an event horizon, which side of it you're on.

Routine is good. It keeps your feet on the ground when your mind is falling into the sky.

I lock and load the coffeemaker every night. Every morning I check the *New York Times* website to make sure official reality has made it through the dark hours. When Julie gets up, she invokes a smaller but no less official reality by logging into her job, which involves editing technical literature for technology companies.

In the summer I cut firewood, repair fence, and engage in the 3Ms of lawn care: maintaining the gasoline-powered sprinkler system, mowing the grass and weeds, and murdering an occasional gopher. In the winter I work on skis—repairing bases, sharpening edges, and waxing according to the forecast. Depending on the season we have dinner on the deck and watch the sun go down behind the peaks at nine, or sit by the woodstove with cups of tea and detective novels after the sun has disappeared into dark snow clouds at four-thirty.

In the kitchen we play to our strengths. Unless I'm making spaghetti, Julie cooks and I do the dishes and clean up the counters. On Tuesdays Julie has yoga class in town, and I ride in with her to sit and talk with a couple of other old guys in the bar next to the yoga studio. We call Tuesday Beer and Yoga Night.

We are still alive. Words for my third-grade teacher. Fifteen years after we moved here to spend our last days in the place we loved, civilization is still sustaining the unsustainable.

We know it all could change in an instant. Great rolling clouds of fire could move down from the lodgepole-thick foothills any August day, or one of us could have an iffy blood test come back from the lab, or a texting driver could drift into our lane when we're driving into town to check the mail. The oceans could turn to purple acid, the Arctic ice cap could melt, the bees and butterflies could all die. Twenty-first-century extermination camps could be in the process of construction, and engineered contagions and nerve gas and nuclear bombs are all out there, waiting for human error or anger.

I think about Julie dying before I do. I think about dying before Julie does. Both of these are good-news/bad-news jokes without the good news.

Julie tells me that I worry too much about things I can't do anything about.

"I'm not worrying," I say. "I'm *thinking*."

"I think you're worrying," she says.

"I only worry about things I *can* do something about," I say. "Then I do something about them. Then I go on and do something about the next thing I worry about, so I don't have to worry about it, either."

"I think you *think* too much about things you can't do anything about," she says.

"But," I say, "extinction."

"Extinction will take care of itself. There are good things left in this world, you know. Think about them."

Good advice, even if I don't always follow it. It's been hard to follow since third grade.

Four times a year—on the equinoxes and solstices—we invite friends in the valley to our house for a celebratory get-together. We gossip and stay up late, but with our crowd that means everybody is home and in bed by midnight, our kitchen is clean, and we have engaged in a small, quiet ceremony of thankfulness that we have good friends who like to talk and laugh with each other.

When you're never sure the world will last through the week, everyday friendships and conversations become the safest parts of your mind.

2

Question: How do you contemplate all the depressing things in this world without threatening your sanity? In other words, how do you stay conscious without getting depressed?

Answer: You don't, at least not at first.

In 1990 the American author William Styron published *Darkness Visible*, an account of a depression that struck him while he was in the midst of literary and financial success. The book is not proof of Styron's eloquence or of his prowess as a thinker, but of his complete failure to articulate what he went through. Again and again his book shows depression as a state of fear and pain without words for fear and pain. It also lacks convincing words for past and future, self and other.

I read *Darkness Visible* twice, once before I had gone through a clinical depression and once after.

As a yet-to-be depressed reader, I admired Styron's skill with words and the scope and variety of his metaphors. I saw how he had created characters that had gone to their doom through their own choices. I thought he had shown what it's like to be depressed, and how you could avoid depression.

In the aftermath of depression, all I could see in his book was its failure to give meaning to the horror of the experience.

Styron's many metaphors are attempts to show what depression feels like. When one metaphor doesn't work, he tries another, which doesn't work either. The book and its author devolve to hollow edifices of words, cardboard-cutout defenses against the unspeakable.

In the end Styron simply says he went mad and then

emerged from madness, wounded but alive. There's a blank and impenetrable barrier between the person he was when depressed and the person he was when writing a book about being depressed.

My own experience was similar. Once I realized I was falling into a depression, I determined to meet it head-on. I would take whatever it had to give and emerge from it stronger. That was like standing on the tracks, waiting for the bullet train to come along and teach me about life.

My metaphors of depression aren't any more enlightening than Styron's, but here are some:

The self, that thing you once regarded as a brilliant, supergiant star, has exhausted its fuel and collapsed in on itself. Now it's infinitely small with infinite gravity, the unwelcome center of the universe.

Everything in your world is silently and endlessly turning to ashes.

A demon resides in your skull, telling you a hundred times a day to kill yourself.

Reality becomes an all-encompassing intolerable stasis marked by a thousand meaningless lifetimes a minute. That doesn't make sense. Little about depression does.

Toward the end of my own madness, when a combination of drugs and cognitive therapy had begun to bring me back into a world I could believe was real, I told my psychiatrist I was well enough to stop taking a tricyclic antidepressant, hoping I could avoid its unpleasant side effects and still live. He thought I was stopping it too soon and talked me into taking it for another thirty days, which in itself indicated that I was beginning to rise out of darkness. Thirty days would have seemed an unendurable eternity a few months before.

I also told him that I was beginning to identify the well-springs of my depression.

Several years before, I had ended a decade-long relationship, one marked by infidelity and magical thinking, practices that had eventually transformed joy into pain.

I had turned forty-one. I had thought I would stop aging at forty. My forty-first birthday came as a shock.

My father had had a series of small strokes, and my mother was showing hoarding behaviors that I feared—correctly, it turned out—were the start of dementia.

A student advisee had killed herself after having been the driver in a single-car accident that killed her boyfriend.

A good, much-loved dog, one I had raised on the trail while working as a wilderness ranger, had been killed by a pickup on the highway. I received a letter from the wife of the driver, saying he had aimed for my dog with his pickup, and that she knew it meant that she and her husband were going to hell. The letter, in all its human and canine permutations, made it difficult for me to see the world as a decent place. After years of not thinking about this incident, I had begun thinking about it again.

Finally, after being promoted to full professor at a small liberal-arts college, I had discovered that I had bought into an existential swindle: I was not going to end up as a beloved Mr. Chips wandering around a green campus imparting wisdom, but as a bored and unhappy Mr. Chips sitting slumped over a cold cup of coffee during fear-and-loathing department meetings, when I wasn't correcting an endless stack of first-year essays in a cramped and stuffy office.

My psychiatrist was impressed with this sad list. He told

me he had never had a patient with as much insight into his depression. I told him he needed more patients who were English professors.

Perhaps I was lucky in that my various hearts of darkness were close, and fresh, and undeniable, but I don't think so. Most people, by the time they're forty-one, have lost friends and pets, have seen their parents approach death's horizon, have worked at dream jobs that turned into nightmares, and have seen signs that they won't be forever young. If my psychiatrist is to be believed, most people have the strength to deny the undeniable. I didn't.

The thirty days went by, and with them my last thirty capsules of tricyclic antidepressant. A short course of Prozac blessed me with a gently euphoric I-don't-give-a-shit attitude toward faculty meetings, student suicides, aging, and death. When the Prozac was gone, the euphoria went away, but I have not forgotten how to be an impartial witness to catastrophe.

It's been almost thirty years since that time. I haven't been depressed again, and I haven't had to use antidepressants again, even as I've had time to think about the many things in the world that I *could* get depressed about rather than the few things I *did* get depressed about.

Depression had left behind a gift, in the form of a crucial and lifesaving shift toward fidelity and honesty.

I arrived back in sanity—as opposed to consensus reality—with an appreciation of how insignificant I am in the totality of things, how little my decisions can affect the world, how beautiful the world is, and how lucky I am to be able to witness it up close. Depression cures malignant narcissism if it lets you live. It cures malignant consensus reality, for that matter.

I understand depression is something you shouldn't wish upon your worst enemy. I know—too well, even if I can't articulate it—how my student advisee who killed herself must have looked forward to death as the end of her grief and pain and emptiness where a self used to be.

But if and when you get back from depression, you understand that the stories you constructed about your life and place in the world were flimsy and flawed contraptions that wouldn't survive a therapist's waiting room. Most of these stories came out of your cultural heritage and failed miserably in their job of keeping you an unalienated actor in the cultural theater. In the case of our civilization, of course, the theater wasn't that good in the first place, and the moment when you broke character wasn't, in retrospect, that much to grieve about.

As a formerly depressed person, and as a person who cared for a parent fading into dementia, I know that depression and dementia are two things harder to face than nonexistence.

Awareness and memory and honest attention to the world: they're everything that makes life worth living.

3

Depression nearly killed me once, and it's killed friends and neighbors and people I went to school with. The only thing that saved me was the knowledge that at some point my life had ceased to be my own property and had become the property of the people who loved me. It takes time to understand that distinction, and you can't understand it at all if nobody loves you.

Although there's not enough love in the world, chances are that somebody loves you, and you shouldn't decide to kill yourself without consulting the person or persons doing the loving. The voice of your depression is going to tell you that they don't love you, but you should ask them if that's true. If they say they love you, believe them and stay alive for them.

That said, let's imagine our civilization as a depressed

person. It has had, for a century at least, solid psychoanalytic reasons to believe that nobody loves it. People depend on it, they see its physical structures as their reality, they survive killing temperatures and infectious illness because of it, but they don't love it.

Give them a chance and they'll try to destroy it. In 1929 Freud wrote in *Civilization and Its Discontents* that human nature and civilization are antagonists. It took just half a decade for the Nazis to prove him right.

As long as we're looking at history: I don't know that November 22, 1963, was the date that America decided to destroy itself, but it was close to that time that the poison was swallowed, the gun stuck in the mouth, the bridge rail released to the sky, the toy pistol waved at the cop, the car aimed between the headlights of the semi. These are all dubious metaphors, of course, for the sad acts of late-stage debt-fueled capitalism. Still, the people who look at the Kennedy assassination and cry conspiracy are not wrong to sense, behind it all, a great and miserable colonial intelligence that decided that living was agony, and it wasn't going to put up with it any longer.

Look at greenhouse-gas concentrations and ice-cap volume loss and accelerating concentrations of wealth and you'll find that it's time to call in grief counselors. You'll see points at which the trajectories of these and many more tragic trends could have been altered toward living rather than dying, toward sustainability rather than exponential growth. That those points were ignored speaks of a great and perverse intelligence behind the decision to die.

Civilization's end will begin a massive die-off of humanity, not unlike the one that happened in Rome when the aqueducts were destroyed and the citizens had to drink from the cholera-infested Tiber. Things we take for granted, like sanitation and food, will cause us to yearn for the good old days of technological frenzy, no matter how destructive or perverse or dead set against human fulfillment we found them to be.

I think we've got ten more years of history before we run out. I should know better than to throw out a deadline. Oil-company executives could suddenly show up at the White House to hand over long-suppressed patents for portable sewage-fueled fusion plants. Genetic advances could allow us to live on thorns, toadflax, kudzu, and cheat grass. Sulfur dioxide could transform the atmosphere into a giant orange sunscreen. We could switch to a solar and geothermal economy and go to a global one-child policy.

But the momentum is all in the other direction.

I don't blame you if you insist that policies will change and that all the unlikely solutions I've listed—and more—will come true.

It's easier to think about the end of civilization without getting depressed if you're over sixty, or if you don't have children, or if your children don't have children.

Ten years, a little more or a little less.

4

One of the great projects of empire is the scrupulous maintenance of the normal. What has gone on will always go on, is the official line. Nothing to see here, is what the cop says as you drive by, even when he's just retrieved a head in a motorcycle helmet from the crotch of a roadside tree. It's important to keep the traffic moving if you're a cop, just like it's important to keep the exchange of goods and services going if you're an empire. Never mind the carnage—it's already factored into the balance sheets.

These summers, things look decidedly normal where Julie and I live. On the highway that fronts our driveway, giant diesel pickups go by every twenty seconds or so, towing trailers full of jet skis or four-wheelers. Quarter-million-dollar motorhomes go by in between them, making literal the real-estate industry's phrase, "Parade of Homes." Cars rented at the Boise Airport follow the motorhomes, signaling to get into the passing lane, attempting to move up a place or two before the oncoming traffic makes a head-on collision inevitable. Packs of motorcycles roar by, ridden by armored riders who look like Imperial stormtroopers. The occasional bicyclist balances between fog line and barrow pit, hoping his bike helmet will protect his skull from the extended mirror of the F-250 that's closing in on him at eighty-five miles per hour.

It's a decades-long debt-and-pension-fueled retirement party for the still-living products of the Baby Boom. It's a horde of old people on the move, heading for the glacial lakes that line the east side of the Sawtooth Mountains. In the small town of Stanley, restaurants and patios are filled with wine drinkers and hors d'oeuvre nibblers. Fly-fishing and hiking equipment shops are thick with browsing customers, and the lawn at the local library is filled with the intent faces of people staring at pictures of their grandchildren on the screens of tablets and laptops.

Young people in Sawtooth Valley in the summer are waiting tables in the restaurants, or driving the boat shuttles across Redfish Lake, or wearing firefighting gear in the grocery checkout line, beer and cheese snacks in their baskets.

It's normal this summer for old people to spend money and young people to work for it. It's normal this summer for old people to think they might coast into that great Gas Station in the Sky on the fumes of a dying economy. It's normal for old people to tip generously in our restaurants, because they know that the young people who are serving them won't get any returns on the FICA tax that is taken from their paychecks, and that the ones who are returning to college in the fall will graduate with debt that cannot be repaid in twenty years, if ever, and that if the young people themselves have kids, they won't be able to afford them. It's normal to think that what remains of the great American horn of plenty is located right here in the middle of Idaho, and it's dribbling out its last few honeyed nectarines and grapes and rib eyes.

5

Every October Julie and I put on gloves, carry large orange plastic bags out to the highway, and pick up the trash that the summer's million tourists have deposited in the barrow pits. Along the empty road we find beer cans, beach towels, life jackets, long strips of truck tires, junk-food wrappers, junk mail, grocery bags, water bottles, car parts, tarps, packing peanuts, used disposable diapers, small boxes full of restaurant leftovers, beach toys, and bruised cameras that, when taken home and fitted with new batteries, never seem to work. We do get the pictures off the camera chips to see if we recognize anybody, but we never do, even though a lot of them are close-up selfies.

We imagine ourselves as alien archeologists on a starship heading back to Tau Ceti, poring over artifacts from a ruined planet, wondering what the creatures in the digital photos talked about as they destroyed their own biosphere before they could live apart from it. "One thing we know is that they were religious," Julie says. "They worshipped plastic."

6

Idaho is a desert getting more so. More than half of some of our national forests have already burned. Sawtooth Valley is one of the few places in the state with an abundance of cool water, so when the temperatures in the lower country get above one hundred degrees Fahrenheit, as they do quite often from June through September, even young people drive up from the lowlands. They fish in the Salmon River and float down it. It's a wild and scenic river, protected because it's been relatively untouched by civilization.

Last August we took our camp chairs to Redfish Lake Lodge to listen to Sunday afternoon music on their lawn. We demarcated a square of grass with a little picnic blanket and put our chairs on it. I went to the bar for margaritas, and Julie headed for the food kiosk for sweet potato fries. We met back at the blanket, which was in the middle of five hundred or so humans by the time the music started. Another five hundred were on the nearby beach.

Then people with tall chairs put them just ahead of us and blocked our view of the singer-songwriter. A half-dozen relatives and a couple of slobbering pit bulls joined them on their giant blanket. Two couples crowded in on our left, saying, "You like babies, don't you?" A single mother with two sullen and sprawling teenagers arrived on our right. Our blanket got sprawled.

We had to leave. The patch of lawn exposed when we folded our blanket disappeared as the people on all sides experienced a sudden people vacuum and rushed to fill it. The singer-songwriter was angry, singing about an old lover who had betrayed her. It was a warm, clear afternoon, so we stowed the chairs and blanket in the car and took our food and drink down the lakeshore, away from the music and the crowds.

A month later the crowds were gone, migrated to lower elevations, gathered in schools and offices, flocking together in lines of cars leading up to the service windows of fast-food restaurants, driving bumper-to-bumper on the interstates, the only evidence of their time at Redfish Lake a series of selfies broadcast from their phones.

When they return next June, we will greet them like cargo cultists. The restaurants will reopen.

But Julie and I will be back on the Redfish beach before that, on skis. January is an open-beach month. The only music in the air will come from the sunlit groaning of the ice that stretches across the lake. We'll ski out on the docks and sit for a few minutes, staring back at the boarded-up lodge, sitting on snowy benches under the skeletal steel supports of packed-away summer awnings. I will think of bare ruined choirs, where late the sweet birds sang.

Powdery spindrifts will dance between the trees where musicians once leaned their instruments. The only blanket on the lawn will be made of snow.

Dock sitting will be a short-term affair. Shadows on the lake surface will shift toward darkness, the cold will seep through our parkas, and we will hear the distant, austere song of the wind. We will contemplate death from hypothermia, which is supposed to be pleasant once you're past the initial stages.

We won't want to get past the initial stages, at least not this winter. Not while our solitude is due to the season and not to civilization's collapse. Not while our savings are worth anything, and not while we can return home to electricity and a wood-pile and a full refrigerator and a computer linked to what's left of our culture. We will turn our skis back down the two-mile track to our car. Fifteen minutes later we'll be putting pieces of fresh-chopped wood on the still-warm embers in the stove.

7

"As you know, there is no such thing as society. There are individual men and women, and there are families." Margaret

Thatcher, the demented prime minister of the United Kingdom, said that in 1987. She still had three years to go as prime minister and eighteen years before her Alzheimer's would be publicly announced by her daughter.

But Thatcher's remark indicates she was already demented in 1987. She was much further along in her dementia in 2004 when she attended, against the advice of her doctors, the funeral of her demented friend Ronald Reagan. Reagan had died that year of Alzheimer's, ten years after he had announced his diagnosis in a farewell speech to the American people. Reagan summed up much of his administration when he said, "They say the world has become too complex for simple answers. They are wrong." That was his Alzheimer's speaking.

One symptom of dementia, from what I've seen of it, is an increasing literal-mindedness. That both Reagan and Thatcher, arguably the two most influential leaders of the late twentieth century, adopted a muscular literality in the face of complex social and ecological issues indicates that dementia begins decades before it shows up as confusion and lost memories. It's no wonder that they both rejected the idea that humanity might be a complex social organism with a collective psyche that needed healing. They saw it instead as an atomized horde of rapacious singletons.

That they both became leaders of their countries suggests that late-stage capitalism temporarily favors those who, because of brain damage on the cellular level, must take its metaphors literally. I'm thinking of debt, or national borders, or religion, or the individual.

I list the individual as a metaphor because for most of humanity's history, individuality has only been an improbable idea, the abstract embodiment of loneliness. For the first quarter-million years of our species, the true human unit was the tribe. A tribe was the way people connected with each other. It was the way they defined who they were. An individual without a tribe was not a person.

During my mother's descent into dementia, it was possible to imagine that the person I knew as my mother was gone, and in her place was a perverse intelligence that took pleasure in asking, again and again, who of her friends and family had died. When she had asked about everyone she could think of, she would declare herself to be the only one left. It was true. Once her husband, sons, friends, and coworkers had been parts of her world. Now, if you left the room after visiting her for an hour or two, she asked if you were dead, too, sometimes to your face. Then she would ask again if her parents were gone. I don't know where the rest of her had disappeared to, but the part that was left had no connection to anyone else and spent all its time wondering where those connections had gone.

It's not an exaggeration to say what makes us human remains our connection to other humans. It's not a metaphor to say that eight billion humans comprise a giant collective organism, one that has a collective intelligence, a collective will, a collective unconscious, and a collective vulnerability to cultural dementia. That's what I would have told Margaret Thatcher and Ronald Reagan, had I been able to talk to them when they were in power. They would have disagreed with me, and Thatcher would have kept transferring to corporations, at a huge loss, the property of generations of British taxpayers, and Reagan would have kept on funneling public money to the defense industry.

If I had asked them why they were doing things that were hurting millions of people in their own countries, they would have grinned vacantly and said, in unison, "They're all gone. I'm the only one left."

8

Maybe we don't need dementia metaphors to explain what's going on in the world. Medical investigators have discovered that the Zika virus can infect the hippocampus of an adult, destroying neuronal stem cells and shrinking the memory-retaining parts of the brain. The discovery gives rise to the suspicion that there are yet more pathogens out there, and that our civilization's burden of dementia cases might not be due to aging alone—it might be the fallout from a viral bioweapon similar to Zika, except that it's been around since 1955, feasting on hippocampus pie, turning idealistic business-school graduates into the sociopathic CEOS of corporations producing cluster bombs or overpriced pharmaceuticals or patented seed stocks. Once that stuff gets in a boardroom, you'll have to burn down the whole building to get rid of it.

Any other non-metaphors? Cultural dementia itself can be depressingly non-metaphoric. Researchers are reporting that chronic traumatic encephalopathy afflicts a majority of ex-football players, even ones who never played in the NFL—high school and college players, in other words. CTE doesn't stem from concussions as much as from small repetitive blows to the head, the kind that can be described as business-as-usual in football. Our educational institutions, which purportedly exist to promote intelligence, are really in the business of destroying memory and abstract thinking in a substantial portion of our population.

One way of looking at late-stage capitalism is that it feeds on human beings no longer capable of abstract thought.

Another way of looking at late-stage capitalism is that in a culture in which an inability to conduct abstract thought is rewarded with promotions and hard cash, it gets harder and harder to detect brain damage.

9

Population is the Ur-problem, according to many of us who have chosen not to have children. We cite the fact that an industrially civilized kid's contribution to atmospheric carbon will dwarf any environmentally aware behavior the kid's extended family could do to offset it.

Over a lifetime, such kids produce exponentially more atmospheric carbon than a diesel pickup, especially if they decide to buy diesel pickups, or if they have children themselves and those children buy diesel pickups, or use electricity, or obtain credit cards and visit big-box stores.

The false assumption behind this thinking is that industrial civilization will survive for several more generations.

Those children will never make it to full consumerhood. It won't matter how many siblings they have. It will matter to their parents, of course, and to the amount of grief accrued in their lifetimes and that of their kids. But on a planetary scale, adding one or two or ten children to eight billion isn't going to change much, especially if the economy has toileted and you can't buy teddy bears or car-sized cartons of disposable diapers. In an organism with eight billion malnourished cells, they won't show up as a trace element.

If having kids doesn't matter, you're not too far from a moral condition where, as in the old song by Cole Porter and Friedrich Nietzsche, "Anything Goes."

Once you've understood the numbers, it's hard to find any decision or effort or person that matters—unless you're looking at a Russian submarine commander contemplating launching a nuclear-armed torpedo at an American aircraft carrier. You hope, then, that there are no Russian submarine commanders who read Nietzsche. You hope that there are no Russian submarine commanders who have been bitten by virus-carrying mosquitos. You hope none of them played football in high school.

Climate change and population growth are already pinching countries into starvation, disease, and civil war. World leaders, facing their own unthinkable demise after a lifetime of wishing their enemies dead, are contemplating taking their enemies with them, which leads to the speculation that the afterlife, if it exists, is probably not an arena of peace and forgiveness. It's probably hot and crowded and full of accusations and denials, and it's about to get more so.

There are people who are planning to survive what's coming, even if it involves nuclear weapons. Some of them are building bunkers and safe rooms not too far from where Julie and I live, and wondering how they're going to ensure the loyalty, or at least obedience, of their security personnel.

If you're one of them, before you spend all your money on a bunker and shock collars for your employees, let me refer you to *The Fate of the Earth*, a book by Jonathan Schell. Schell is a meticulous researcher if a ponderous writer, and he ponderously and meticulously demonstrates that no one, even the most well-equipped survivalist, can survive even a small nuclear war.

He also spends a long chapter mourning the death of human consciousness. I, too, mourn the death of consciousness, especially when it happens in people still walking around underground, inspecting their diesel-powered freezers and wondering if the new cook will try stealing a prime rib like the old one did.

But Jonathan Schell's mourning causes a bit of cognitive dissonance. You start thinking that if there's no consciousness to mourn the death of consciousness, what's the problem?

For Schell, the problem is that consciousness exists for

its own sake, as a unique, once-in-a-planet's-lifetime thing. Nuclear war would end that thing once and for all.

Schell doesn't get into the other things that are ending consciousness, such as a civilization that has literalized its metaphors for depression and dementia. That is, we're silently and endlessly turning the world into ashes. And we've become convinced that we're individual human beings, each one of us the only one left.

These things are the cognitive equivalent of nuclear war. They kill consciousness, just as surely as would ten thousand nuclear weapons detonating in the biosphere.

10

Shortly after my sixty-fifth birthday, I used the stairs to arrive at my physician's office for my initial Medicare physical.

It was the beginning of a long string of improbable realizations:

> I had experienced above-ground nuclear testing in the American West and was still above ground. I hadn't sucked in one of the particles of plutonium that were dancing around Ketchum Elementary School in the 1950s.

> I'd been insured long enough to develop a relationship with a doctor, which implied a functional medical industry.

> I still had enough of my wits about me to show up at a clinic at an appointed time.

> There was still a clinic.

> My culture still valued old people enough to supply some of them with insurance.

There still existed a hierarchy of knowledge, and the people with medical degrees still had offices and still received money from Medicare.

I still had the strength and agility to take the stairs instead of the elevator.

And because all of the above *was* improbable—it meant that there were great numbers of people for whom none of it was true.

It also meant that whatever data my physician took from my session became a set of baselines from which my decline was more or less guaranteed. But such data linked me to a vast system of preventative procedures and ameliorative chemistry that made it likely that, should civilization stay alive long enough, I would reach eighty. At that point, if I had finally witnessed the death of American civilization, I would be too old to demand sympathy for a much-shortened life.

My physician drew my blood, thumped on my back and belly, tested my reflexes, looked at the whites of my eyes, asked me how I'd been sleeping, checked my toenails to see that I'd still been able to bend over far enough to trim them, and, finally, burned actinic keratoses off my face with liquid nitrogen. He pronounced me good for another year.

Then, as he was about to leave and attend to his next patient, he asked me if there was anything new in my life, and I told him that Julie and I had gotten a new puppy. He gave me a big smile, which was remarkable because he was normally reserved and precise and not professionally inclined to give his patients reason for long-term optimism.

"Getting a puppy," he said, "is one of the best things you can do for your health-span."

He said health-span instead of life-span because he knew there were worse things than death. At my age, another clinical depression or a diagnosis of Alzheimer's, for example, would be the end of my health-span.

"Puppies make you get out and exercise," he said. "They make you laugh. They make you crawl around on the floor cleaning up puppy messes. They lower your blood pressure. They take your mind off the terrible things you can't do anything about."

Everything he said was true. Exercise keeps you healthier longer, and when puppies want to go with you when you go for a hike or a ski, they let you know. You start feeling guilty if you don't take them. They jump and growl and shake their leashes and stand between you and the door, and also between you and thoughts of dying oceans and child soldiers being forced, as a hazing ritual, to kill their parents.

It occurred to me that Juno—that's our puppy's name—and I would have about the same amount of future, if she didn't get out on the highway in front of a pickup, and if I, digging a posthole, didn't stir up and breathe in the leftovers from a 1962 atomic test over the border in Nevada. Julie has a couple of decades more if the actuarial tables hold true and if things hold together far longer than expected.

But it's certain that in the next decade the world is going to be filled with a never-ending grief as climate catastrophes and wars and too many refugees all happen at once. Elizabeth Kubler-Ross says that the final stage of grief is acceptance, but in my instance the acceptance has brought the realization that when you're looking at the last gasps of humanity, acceptance is only the start of grief.

Our puppy became our metaphor for a fragile, beautiful, short-lived world, one full of terror and tragedy, but one that is worth nurturing and being kind to. It is possible, in such a world, to have a kind of puppy-scale morality, where the peaks that surround our valley become an ethical horizon. You focus on the small things in front of you, the things you can do something about. You feed the puppy and groom her and make sure she pees outside and not on the rug. You try to lead by example. You make sure she's safe, because she's your best defense against a grief you can't see the end of.

It's a matter of turning attention away from the hopeless to the hopeful. It's a dive into a benign literalism, a kind of killed-virus inoculation against the malignant literalities of depression and dementia and the strange, alien intelligences that speak through them.

Right now, Juno, no longer a puppy but acting like one, is growling and shaking her rope. I'm pretty sure her rope is her metaphor for a squirrel. It would be, anyway, if she wasn't afraid of squirrels.

Also, we are expecting friends for our end-of-summer dinner. The table is set. Wineglasses sit on folded napkins. I've swept the floor and vacuumed the rugs. Soon, people will arrive with wine and covered dishes. Potlucks are happy occasions in Sawtooth Valley, where the lack of restaurants in the winter makes for well-practiced cooks. I'm making spaghetti.

Juno and her rope and our potluck may seem trivial in the face of a biosphere becoming toxic. You might think I should be spending my time looking for solutions to ongoing extinctions. But looking for solutions where none exist is trivial in itself.

It's more important to remain a careful and conscious witness to the good things that humans still embody. Those are love, kindness, empathy, and caring. They don't seem to work well at the scale of billions of people. They work better if you can exercise them when folks are over for dinner.

People must have had the same thoughts in Roman villas above the Mediterranean during the summer of the year 400. Or on the river in Baghdad in the early fall of 1256. Or in sumptuous homes outside of Constantinople in 1450. Or in London, at a pre-theater fete on a darkening evening in 1914, the war barely begun.

Guests must have brought food and wine and the evenings must have been full of talk and laughter. It must have seemed to those hosts that summers would always return, and guests would always be kind and conscious and intelligent people, bearing gifts.

acknowledgments

Previous iterations of portions of this book first appeared as guest essays on Guy McPherson's doomsday blog *Nature Bats Last*, where I first noticed that people could intellectually grasp the end of civilization, while avoiding its emotional realities, sometimes violently. That phenomenon has given purpose to my writing, which these days attempts to drive home the personal implications of collapse. I am grateful to Dr. McPherson for his books and his blog, which gave me the space and the impetus to first sketch out my own response to the unsustainable.

Earlier versions of some chapters have appeared in anthologies published by the Dark Mountain Project in Great Britain:

"When Darkness Casts a Hard and Pitiless Light" was published in Issue 2 (Summer 2011) of the series as "Consensus and Other Realities."

"Resort Life" was published in Issue 3 (Summer 2012) as "Last Days, Last Words."

"The Unconscious and the Dead" was published in Issue 4 (Summer 2013).

"The Way We Live Now" was published in Issue 8 (Autumn 2015) as "Life and Love after Collapse."

"The Way We Live Now, Again" was published in Issue 11 (Spring 2017) as "The Way We Live Now: The Metaphors of Extinction."

"The Unconscious and the Dead" was re-anthologized in a 2017 Chelsea Green publication, *Walking on Lava: Selected Works for Uncivilized Times*.

Additionally, "A Few Rocks from the Box" was published in *High Desert Journal* in the Fall 2010 issue, and "Vietnam as Simulacrum" was published in the 2019 edition of the *Limberlost Review*.

Bits and pieces of the book were first published in my columns in the *Idaho Mountain Express* and *Boise Weekly*.

I am deeply grateful to the University of New Mexico Press and its director, Stephen Hull, for giving me the opportunity to gather all this material together in one volume, focus it in the direction of the everyday human, and see it published before the end of the world.

I am, in advance, just as grateful to my readers. I hope my thoughts will represent misplaced pieces of the puzzle for them, and that they'll forgive me for the complexities and paradoxes those thoughts introduce to the big picture.